Defeat Your Saboteurs

Devils,
Demons
& Unclean
Spirits In
A Fallen
World

T. Grant Acker

Cover Photo by Michelle Monique Photography

FIRST EDITION

ISBN: 978-1-936989-87-4

Library of Congress Control Number: 2012918360

Published by
NewBookPublishing.com, a division of Reliance Media, Inc.
515 Cooper Commerce Drive, #140, Apopka, FL 32703
NewBookPublishing.com

Printed in the United States of America

Table Of Contents

The fact that I am writing this proves that God has a huge sense of humor and that He chooses who He will for the purpose of showing His love.

Special thanks to: Jesus DePaz, Manuel Cruz, Michele Trapp, Kristine Smith, Susane Plaza and the unknown people who have prayed much for me.

Fellow Traveler Timothy.

Introduction

Think Radical. If you were born with a spiritual silver spoon in your mouth you probably don't need this book. But, if your life is not great, or if it downright *sucks*, this book is for you.

I am not a religious person, this book is not about religion, it is about a very real encounter with a very real (and only true) God. He was the last guy I figured was relevant to my life, but He is by far the best friend I have ever had. That very real and true God has made a way for you to have a good and full life (abundant). Taking and living that abundant life that God has opened for mankind through Jesus (John 10:10) is what this book is about.

This book is not about theology, it is about what God has taught me to climb (still climbing) out of the hole in which I was born. I am probably on the outer fringe of everything (try me), but in order to teach *you* what *you* need to know, I may sound mainline…that is for *your* benefit. The point is, stay with this book, read it, keep it at hand, use it to encourage and help you as you take a new and full life; but beware, the devil will make sure to send you religious persons (even some Christian leaders) to dispute the "theology" of this book. You have nothing to lose by accepting and applying what is taught in this book...and much to lose: the life God has for you and perhaps your health and physical life. Don't give up the hope that God will show you in this book – read it, use it and take what Jesus has for you.

The *truth* is that through Jesus Christ, and specifically His death on the cross, you have access to an <u>entirely</u> new life. To get and live that life it is necessary to know God, know about God, how and why He works and the very real *multidimensional* environment (as in spirit dimension) in which you live. God wants you to learn how to manage and control the negative, tragic, evil forces that work against you on a daily basis so you can eliminate or reduce the crummy parts of your life. He wants you to receive and enjoy His provision for the promised abundant good life.

Life is not good when it's filled with loss, fear, torment, temptation, lust and sin. All of these things have a spiritual connection not with God but with the "powers and principalities" of darkness. They are manifestations of evil.

This book is in five parts. The first focuses on understanding your spiritual environment and your enemies. The second is about God and what He did to give you a new life. The third section deals with faith: what it is and how it works.

The fourth section talks about grasping the *mind blowing*, more-fantastic-than-fiction life that God has opened for you, and the fifth contains specific tools to acquire that good and abundant life.

I develop the theme in stages. Be patient, even if you are expert in an area; to get to the end that God has for you, you must understand the foundations. The beginning is to know that *like it or not, believe it or not, there is a genuine spirit realm that controls much of your existence and always impacts you for good and for ill.* The Holy Bible says you are a human spirit temporarily living in a biodegradable body with a soul. This book deals with human existence on all levels in which you live – spirit, soul and body.

This book is <u>not only about telling</u>. This book is also <u>about showing you</u> how, in Christ Jesus, to access and live the promised good and abundant life that God has opened for you. Within these pages, I offer hard won *knowledge, understanding, and tools.* The Bible says that "God's people perish for lack of knowledge." (Hosea 4:6(a)

If you'll open your heart to this information, then God will confirm it for you. You will then have to exercise your faith and take what God has given you. The Bible says: "Who has believed our report? And to whom has the arm of the LORD been revealed?" Isaiah 53:1

The more traumatized you are—the harder your life has been, the lonelier you are—the more you'll need to know, understand and act upon to live an abundant life, and the deeper you'll have to dive into every area of your life. *The greater the wounding, the greater the healing…if you will understand and embrace it.* It won't be easy, but you *will* move forward into abundance even though there will be losses, too…just know that at the end, heaven awaits you.

In this fallen world, there seem to be countless "realities," but God wants you to lay claim to the one He carved out especially for you as a result of the life and death of His Son—a life that offers eternal life, security, health, sanity and goodness.

Fasten your seat belts. It's gonna be a bizarre ride – even mind boggling, but I promise it's worth it.

Note: I see that some parts of this book have been influenced by my experience ten years ago with and through the very good book: <u>Christ the Healer</u>, by John G. Lake. As far as I know there are no direct quotes, but in certain parts there is influence from certain sections of his book that have been confirmed in my own experience with Jesus.

Spirit World

What you are: spirit, soul and body

You are an eternal spirit and soul presently residing within a biodegradable human body. Your soul had its genesis the moment your spirit entered your physical body. While you remain in your body, your spirit, and soul are fused together.

Your soul is where your emotions, intelligence and will reside. The Bible describes your soul as its own entity, but experience, science, and the Bible also indicate that your soul is fused to your spirit and to your body for as long as you live. Your soul remains with your spirit when you die; that is, you remain "who" you are even after what we commonly call "death." This is revealed in 1 Sam 28: 14 – 19; after death, Samuel is still Samuel; he knows and remembers King Saul.

From the moment of your rebirth in Christ, your soul is in the process of being transformed through the presence of God within you.

Your spirit has a form. It isn't something that just floats in the air. To my spiritual eyes, it appears a little larger than the human body and, I suspect, is what some people call an "aura." Your spirit moves and your body follows, taking its cues from your spirit.

Your body needs no introduction. You need to consciously realize, though, that in its natural state it craves things and activities that aren't good for it, your soul or your spirit.

Biblical examples of the human spirit

When God didn't answer King Saul's inquiries concerning the coming battle with the Philistines (I Samuel, chapter 28), the spirit of the prophet Samuel was called up from the grave. Samuel (his spirit, or ghost if you prefer) had form and senses. Samuel was able to perceive Saul, knew where he was, and also knew what would happen. His spirit body had ears, eyes, arms, legs, intelligence, etc. (Samuel was Samuel.)

The very odd appearance of Moses and the strange prophet Elijah (both long dead) with Jesus on a mountain (labeled with the cool name "The Mount of Transfiguration") is another account of the existence of the spirit body as a specific form. Jesus' disciples (Peter, James and John) saw Moses and Elijah speaking with Jesus. To accommodate their presence Peter, on sensory overload and without a clue as to what to say, offered to make shelters for them (Matthew 17:1–4).

The spirit is the key. It is your spirit that animates you in the physical realm. Your physical body is the vehicle (think personal automobile) that gives you direct access to the physical part of this planet. Your physical body doesn't continue as a viable entity without the animating influence of your spiritual body – it just returns to dirt.

Note, your spirit body has ears and eyes made of spirit. Your spirit body can listen, see and understand what is happening in the spirit world. **God's plan is for the Holy Spirit, joined with your spirit, to prudently direct you.** Your spirit, strengthened by God's presence, aware and awake in God, and quickened to action by God's desires, is to direct your soul and physical body.

In the natural world, without the presence of the indwelling God (that is the God of the Bible living inside a person), a body and/or soul will direct itself to satisfy its own natural desires. It is also amazingly common for a person to have at least one indwelling spirit (a spirit in rebellion to God living inside). Depending on the strength of invading spirits, these beings can direct a person by influencing his or her mind, emotions, and body. In some cases they have complete control of a person.

Two Worlds

You live in two worlds (or dimensions): physical (also known as natural) and spiritual.

1. The natural world is what you can see, discern and/or touch with your natural eyes and other physically-grounded senses.

2. The spirit world is where your spirit lives (presently encapsulated in a human body); it's the dimension where God, the angels of God and fallen angels live. The spirit world is made of a spirit substance; it has geography and spirit material. You can't see it with natural eyes.

Both dimensions are controlled by laws. In the physical world, all things are governed by natural laws (e.g., the law of gravity). The same applies to specific laws that govern the spirit world.

In the natural world, everything has an ending. All things decay because sin entered the world.

In the spirit world, spirit beings exist forever. Spirit beings—angels good and fallen (devils) and the spirits of human beings—have eternal existence.

"Life," in biblical terms, is not the same as eternal existence. All human spirits have eternal *existence*. "Life" refers to being connected to God. Given this understanding, outside of God no one has Life. God wants you to enter into a personal relationship with Him; He wants you to fuse yourself to Him, to become one with Him to receive Life.

Originally, God intended humans to have eternal life in their physical bodies. This was so you and I could enjoy all the wonders of a perfectly-joined spiritual and physical world. Look at the magnificent beauty and diversity of the present world which God created for us… and then imagine how much better it would look and function if it were submitted entirely to its Creator, each part functioning exactly as it was designed. The over the top Old Testament (Bible) prophet Isaiah said that there will be no evil/bad or harm when the knowledge of God covers the earth like water.

When Mankind chose his own way (sin) instead of God's ways, we brought spiritual and physical death into the world (separation from Life and its Source). Sin (evil, harm and death) entered into and penetrated all creation, the animals and the earth.

Christ came from heaven to make it possible for you and me to reconnect with God. In this way, Christ rescued us and brought Life to us again. There is no other way to receive Real Life because it is not a *thing*; it is a *relationship*, it is **unity with God**. The only way to unite with God is through Jesus Christ.

Everyone has eternal existence, but without Christ we will spend eternity separated from God.

Manifestations of The Spirit Dimension

Please stay with me a little longer here; you need to know these things with clarity. Following are relatively brief Biblical passages regarding the spirit dimension and its inhabitants.

Angels of God

The Jews threw Peter in jail because he was preaching the gospel. While in prison (Acts 12:7) the Bible reports: "...an **angel** of the Lord stood by him, and a light shone in the prison; and he struck Peter on the side and raised him up, saying, 'Arise quickly' and his chains fell off his hands."

Evil spirits (demons)

Acts 16:16: "Now it happened, as we went to prayer, that a certain slave girl possessed with a **spirit of divination** met us, who brought her masters much profit by fortune telling. This girl followed Paul and us, and cried out, saying,

'These men are the servants of the Most High God, who

proclaim to us the way of salvation.' And this she did for many days. But Paul, greatly annoyed, turned and said to the **spirit**, 'I command you in the name of Jesus Christ to come out of her.' And he came out that very hour."

Luke 8:27 – 29: "And when He stepped out on the land, there met Him a certain man from the city who had demons for a long time. And he wore no clothes, nor did he live in a house but in the tombs. When he saw Jesus, he cried out, fell down before Him, and with a loud voice said, 'What have I to do with You, Jesus, Son of the Most High God? I beg You, do not torment me!' For He had commanded the unclean spirit to come out of the man."

Luke 9:42 re: the power of demons:

"…the demon threw him down and convulsed him."

Examples of seeing the Spirit World

2 Kings, 6:16 & 17

"So he answered, 'Do not fear, for those who are with us are more than those who are with them [a physical army]' and Elijah prayed, and said, 'Lord, I pray, open his eyes that he may see.' Then the Lord opened the eyes of the young man, and he saw. And behold the mountain was full of horses and chariots of fire all around Elisha."

Acts 7:55

"But he, being full of the Holy Spirit, gazed into heaven and saw the glory of God, and Jesus standing at the right hand of God..."

Example of seeing, hearing and communicating with the Spirit World

Acts 9:3 "...as he journeyed he came near Damascus, and suddenly a **light shone around him from heaven**. Then he fell to the ground and **heard** a voice saying to him, 'Saul, Saul, why are you persecuting me?' And **he said**, 'Who are You, Lord?' Then the **Lord said**, 'I am Jesus, whom you are persecuting."

The spirit world is real and exists alongside the natural world. You must believe, know, and understand that there *is* a spirit world, know certain things about it, and what was (and is) done in it to receive what God has for you.

The Supernatural

The supernatural has control of, or influence over, the natural world through spiritual laws, "stuff" made of spirit material, and spirits (either God's or Satan's) and by events in the spirit world.

God works supernaturally. He changes the results of natural laws with his power.

Satan works supernaturally, too. Acts 8:11 reveals that Simon the sorcerer did great magic and "astonished the people." The Book of Revelation relates that greater works of Satan will manifest in the future.

There is a constant flow between the natural and spiritual dimensions, from the spirit to the physical and from the physical to the spiritual.

Because you are a spirit living in a physical body, you live in both worlds and are subject to natural and supernatural forces. These forces, combined with your will, control 100% of your life.

There is no escape from the spirit world and the influence of the supernatural over your life. There is no safe place. You can't opt out; to deny its existence has no effect. Denying the existence of the spiritual and supernatural, or believing in other things, doesn't change the reality of the spirit world or diminish its influence over your life. Your environment is defined by God, who made it for your good, and by the consequences of sin that brought corruption.

The good news (Gospel) is that God has given you, as a believer, authority and power over the spirit world and its powers (ruling spirit beings); that is, over the spiritual and supernatural influences of evil. Even without Christ, our *human will* blocks entrance of many harmful things into our lives. But in Christ we are given *far greater authority* over what Satan can deliver to us.

Luke 10:17&19:

"...even the demons are subject to us in Your [Jesus'] name."

"Behold, I give you the *authority* to trample on serpents and scorpions, and over all the power of the enemy, and nothing shall by any means hurt you."

To orient yourself properly, knowledge of the spirit and natural world is essential. It's imperative that you know about God and about the enemy so you know how to receive from God and how to fight Satan and his hosts of evil spirits.

Manifestations of the power and influence of the supernatural can be great or not very noticeable, but they are with you 100% of the time.

One dramatic biblical manifestation is found in Daniel in the story of Shadrach, Meshach and Abed-Nego, three young captives from Israel. King Nebuchadnezzar constructed a huge idol and gave orders that all would worship it. The three young men disobeyed the king's orders on the basis of their knowledge of the real God.

Chapter 3, verses 21 – 27 of Daniel states: "Then these men were bound in their coats, their trousers, their turbans, and their other garments, and were cast into the midst of the burning fiery furnace. Therefore, because the king's command was urgent, and the furnace exceedingly hot, the flame of the fire killed those men who took up Shadrach, Meshach and Abed-Nego. And these three men, Shadrach, Meshach and Abed-Nego, fell down into the midst of the burning fiery furnace. Then King Nebuchadnezzar was astonished; and he rose in haste and spoke, saying to his counselors, 'Did we not cast three men bound into the midst of the fire?' They answered and said to the king, 'True, O king.' 'Look !' he answered, 'I see four men loose, walking in the midst of the fire; and they are not hurt, and the form of the fourth is like the son of God.' Then Nebuchadnezzar went near the mouth of the burning fiery furnace and spoke, saying, 'Shadrach, Meshach and Abed-Nego, servants of the Most High God, come out, and come here.' Then Shadrach, Meshach and Abed-Nego came from the midst of the fire. And the satraps, administrators, governors, and the king's counselors gathered together, and they saw these men on whose bodies the fire had no power; the hair on their head was not singed nor were their garments affected, and the smell of the fire was not on them."

Another manifestation of the supernatural is found in I Kings 18:31–38 in the history of Elijah and the prophets of Baal.

An example of the supernatural power of Jesus (God) is found in John 9:6 & 7, where a man born blind has his sight restored.

You live in both worlds: the natural world—what you can

see with your eyes, touch with your hands or smell with your nose—and the spirit world, where your spirit lives. There are natural forces and supernatural forces. As the above passages show, supernatural forces affect or move the natural *apart* from the laws that govern the natural world.

And it's not just the spirit world that affects you in the natural world; the physical world also affects your spirit world. According to Luke 10:17&19: "Then the seventy returned with joy, saying, 'Lord, even the demons are subject to us in Your name.' 'Behold I give you the authority to trample on serpents and scorpions, and over all the power of the enemy, and nothing shall by any means hurt you.' "

Using the authority God gives you, you can stop Satan in his tracks by what you say and do. Words have substance and spiritual meaning. With your mouth, you can overcome and defeat the enemy. The Bible says what we bind (or loose) on earth we also bind (or loose) in heaven (Matthew 19:19).

According to the Bible, the Word of God is spirit. One of the most powerful weapons you have is to speak the Word of God out loud in faith. The Word of God is a spirit thing that stops and even cuts the enemy; it also separates what is godly within you from the world and the enemy. You can't fight the spirits with flesh and bone or other physical weapons: they don't have a physical body. You fight them with prayer, with the Word of God, with your actions and words, and by exerting your authority

<u>over them and over the spirit world.</u> The quality of your life will depend on what you do in this regard.

Things Made of Spirit

In the same way there are material things, there are spirit things: annoyance, blame, sadness and sickness are examples of spirit things. There is of course an emotional, mental and physical aspect to these things, especially in the case of sickness – but understand, there is also a spiritual part. These "things" are spirit burdens which Satan wants to put on and in you; they also open doors so he has greater access to you. Often they are a pervasive, specific emanation from an evil spirit, but even without a spirit being present, spirit things have an ongoing influence and active role.

Did you notice the parallel between the physical and spiritual dimensions? *In both, there are things, consequences to actions, and beings.*

Even walls can have spirit stuff lodged inside

I preached fairly often in a Mexican church where sin and unhappiness had occurred in the pastor's family and church. The hurt, pain, suffering and consequences of sin had become lodged in the walls; they emanated despair, unhappiness and a sense of evil to all those who entered. The pastor and I, and later the pastor alone, spent a year casting those spirit things out of the walls. During that time, he also anointed the building everywhere with oil, following each anointing with prayer. It took an entire year before people could enter the building without feeling sad, uncomfortable, etc. The attacks and the sin that had occurred left a residue. We also anointed the people and preached healing during the year. After every service, the people would come forward and cry. A year later they were well—healed—and the pastor stopped the healing services. Healthy life resumed. He began to minister to the congregation in other ways.

A positive example of spirit "things" are spiritual gifts. These are actual "things" (gifts) that the Lord gives each of us. Like negative spirit things, they have an ongoing role in the life of believers. In the case of spiritual gifts, each is in part a manifestation of the Spirit of God (I Cor. 12:1) and in part they are deposits which operate in certain ways. Spiritual gifts include faith, miracle working, prophecy, discernment of spirits, gifts of healings, etc. (I Cor. 12:8–10).

The Spirit World Is Real and Orderly

In the same way there are natural laws which control the natural world, there are spiritual laws that control the spirit world. Cause and effect also exist in the spirit world. The spirit world moves in accordance to law and what God, Satan *and you and I* do.

In the spirit world live "persons" made purely of spirit. There are angels of God, fallen angels that serve the devil, and there is God. All are visible to each other within the spirit world.

There are also "things," as in the natural world. In the natural world, things are composed of physical material. In the spirit world, things are made of spirit material. Joy, sadness, love, madness, depression and death are examples of spirit things. The Kingdom of God, the work of the cross and salvation also exist in the spirit world and are visible in the spirit world.

Through acts in the natural and spirit worlds, God achieved salvation for you and me through Jesus Christ. This salvation connects us to God and makes us heirs to all that God has for his sons and daughters.

Key points about the spirit world

- The spirit world is not random.
- There are spiritual laws that govern the spirit world in the same way there are natural laws that govern the natural world.
- The spirit world is orderly.
- The spirit world is as real as this world (but not more real).
- It is logical.
- As God honors, created and respects natural laws, so He honors created and respects spiritual laws.
- The laws that govern both worlds work in such a way that there is interchange between the two.
- Actions in one world (dimension) affect the other.
- There is a law, that of faith, which increases the exchange between the two worlds.
- Adam was able to walk and communicate freely with God, consciously living in both worlds.
- The introduction of sin changed the spirit world and the physical world.
- All human beings are subject to both worlds.
- In Christ Jesus we jump from the regular application of the laws (physical and spiritual) to the rules established by and through what Jesus did.

Satan's Plan

Dementia: Disorientation as to time, person, or place

The work of Satan is to prevent you and others from knowing (1) what you are (human spirits in a physical body), (2) that you exist for eternity, (3) that there is a spirit dimension, (4) how the spirit dimension (world) functions, (5) who God is, (6) what Christ did for you on the cross, (7) who you are in Christ (children of God), (8) what God has given you, (9) what God has for you as co-heir of His Kingdom (with and through Christ), and (10) how to get it.

The devil and his confederates act to keep you ignorant or deceived concerning the reality of your existence, and their existence, and the truth about God. They work to disorient you as to time, place, and yourself in relation to everything and especially to God to prevent you from understanding and receiving what God has for you.

Evil is planned and organized. It spans generations. Satan has a plan for everyone's life that began generations ago. Just as we inherit physical DNA, we inherit spiritual DNA. Just as we inherit a physical body, we inherit a spiritual life (but not a spirit; our spirit is created by God). For example, previous generations' addiction to alcohol often results in a lack of spiritual covering (spiritual holes), opens doors to alcoholism, and perhaps allows alcohol spirits (demons) to inhabit unborn babies. I suspect that these factors, together with the devil's power, even affect and change our physical DNA. Notice Satan's power through Pharaoh's magicians (Exodus 7:22 & Ex 8:7).

Ungodly spirit-fed family habits are passed to succeeding generations. Relationships are arranged, often through lust, so children are born with complementary forms of spiritual covering deficits, opening doors to evil and indwelling demons. Much of what we call genetic defects, inherited mental illness, etc. are in truth the presence of spirits and the results of planned evil.

I have observed many times that attention deficit disorder is actually demonic distraction disorder. Learning disabilities are often caused by blocking spirits that limit learning. (See Luke 11:14, where the mute spirit keeps an otherwise healthy person from speaking. See also Luke 9:45 where a spirit hides something (limits understanding.)

Evil spirits usually hide themselves and their work (few would accept them or their ways otherwise) ***and are rarely identified as what they truly are.***

Evil spirits speak, act and move in the unseen realm of the spirit dimension to prevent you from understanding the way existence is structured, how it is governed, your situation in it, and what God has done to save, help and defend you in this fallen world.

When a person knows Christ, Satan makes every effort to

break the relationship between him or her and Christ. In the process, he does everything he can to keep the believer from understanding who he or she belongs to (God), who he or she is (a loved child of God), and the specifics of what can be done to defend against spiritual sabotage.

Remember: Satan comes to rob, kill and destroy; he does everything possible to *ruin your life* (and to keep it from being fixed). When he's unable to reach areas of a person's life, he'll content himself by keeping the person ineffective against him and his confederates. There is nothing good and kind in the kingdom of the devil. Only pure evil exists there, although it's usually well-disguised. (Satan masquerades as an angel of light.) See II Corinthians 11:14.

As you move through life, Satan moves ahead of you, implementing his plan. He speaks evil of you and causes you to feel unable to be happy. He "speaks" by putting thoughts into your mind. He plans and creates situations for you to fall into to make your life difficult and unpleasant. He carries sickness, problems and curses in his hands and does everything possible to dump them on you. He also tries to reach you and your loved ones through access holes and doors that exist in your spiritual coverings.

The correct way to understand evil is to know that the devil's spirits (fallen angels) are unseen (with the natural eye), evil enemies whose purpose is to use God's creation for evil pleasure and then destroy it. You're a target!

Evil's desire is to reach adults and families. These are invisible spirits who are intelligent creative beings (not ghosts of human beings); they're organized and armed with plans and weapons sufficient to rob, kill and destroy.

The spirits come and go at will wherever they choose *unless* they are impeded (by you or someone else); merely *ignoring* them is not enough. They are out to get you; out to win.

They are hateful, selfish entities with a terminal communicable disease (sin). They woo (tempt) you, dance with you, make things seem good even as they infect and destroy you.

After death, you will see them as they are: evil enemies who hide the truth and seduce and destroy. But by then it will be too late to alter course if you've been with them all along. You will be judged and blocked from entry into heaven.

There are different levels of wickedness in evil spirits (Luke 11:26). All are evil, all are in rebellion to God, and all want you to accompany them to hell, but not all are murdering (physical) or horrible insanity-inducing spirits. There are, for example, religious spirits (originally created by God for a holy purpose) who will make you feel good in religious acts and religions that will not save you or lead you to salvation. Note the false "peace" spirits of the Buddhist religion.

Never think that God is evil because he is allowing the presence and the work of the enemy. Satan is legally on earth due to the decision mankind made. It was mankind who chose to "know" good and evil. In tempting Jesus, Satan said to Him, "All this authority [over all the kingdoms of earth] I will give to You, and their glory, for this has been delivered to me...." What has happened and what is happening is not because of God's wrath or desire, but our own decisions. This world mostly reflects man's will, not God's.

God is not double-minded or confused, manifesting Himself through various conflicting religions. Satan, the imposter god, is evil, a polluter and father of lies. He's the creator of confusion and the many false paths to "god", which are really only pathways to fallen angels. (In I Corinthians 8:5, Paul speaks of the many so-called "gods.")

Satan's unpardonable sin was that he wanted to be God. For this reason he was cast out of true heaven. Our triune God (God the Father, Son and Holy Spirit) is the only true God; good and holy are perfect descriptions.

The battle between all false religions, philosophies, systems is over to whom and what you will give your life. They disagree with each other; but all agree on one big lie: Jesus is not God. They say that Jesus is either: crazy, a prophet, a good person, a "spirit," the "Christ spirit," etc. —anything but Who He actually is: God in the flesh who came from heaven (an actual place of unexplainable magnificence) to remove the barrier between God and man.

To say that Jesus is God denies Satan his own "gods" and systems. Loving and obeying God is the ultimate rejection of the devil; by doing so, you define Satan as the loser and imposter he is. Any acceptance of his lieutenants as gods keeps him on the throne since they serve him.

The enemy within – spirit power

Satan's hope and purpose—through every religion, system, philosophy, belief and sin—is to place spirits inside you. The presence of spirits in people is extremely common.

The location and work of the spirit varies depending on the type of spirit and its plan. There are local spirits, including lust, which normally resides in the genital area, and pride, which resides in the throat (so it can speak). Intellectual spirits dwell in the mind. Fear usually lives in the stomach area (even the world recognizes this: "Don't feed fear.")

Spirits can exert their control locally. For example, lust spirits make the genitals hungry for touch and activity. They continue to stimulate the genitals, trying to move their victims to action.

At some point most, if not all, of the spirits attempt to hijack some part of the mind. When they do, actually occupying the brain area or directly connecting to it, their very presence gives them a part in the way the person acts: they'll participate in the personality and intentions of the victim. They'll also serve as a *filter* to everything the victim perceives. For example, a spirit of rejection will color words and deeds so that its victim will perceive everything coming his or her way as signifying rejection. An evil spirit sabotages your mind's ability to interpret information from a true, undefiled, static-free perspective. Another part of evil spirits' purpose is to convince you of the "truth" of their doctrine, by "witnessing" to their "truth."

This can be so extreme that the person changes greatly. For example, a chaste person with a lust spirit (perhaps generational) will say and do things when the spirit is in control that the person would never do on his/her own. There truly are multiple persons inside the body: the person and the spirit (or spirits). In the case of lust, when the body is satisfied the lust spirits loses control and the human person suffers remorse and shock.

Through the action of the above, cultures and sub-cultures are defined, in part, by the type of spirits that are most active in that group of people. In homosexual and single communities there are specific types of fornication spirits occupying people's minds to suggest pleasurable experiences outside the established (ordained, holy, matrimonial) use of the body. Fornication spirits also "testify" that homosexuality, unmarried, recreational sex and other kinds of sexual expression are acceptable when in truth they are contrary to God's standards.

Comments on inheritance

Along with the foregoing, the concept of inheritance

answers at least part of the oft-asked question: Why do bad things happen to good people and good things to bad people? (Jeremiah 12:1b). A bad person may have inherited wealth, good looks, wisdom, discretion, intelligence, athletic skill, and talent. The inheritance from generations past, the business success of a grandfather, "good" marriages, life skills, etc., may well manifest in such a person so that everything he or she does prospers because the person is prepared in all areas of life, even though he or she is a bad or even evil person. The presence of business spirits and pride spirits, and/or the absence of certain classes of hindering spirits, can contribute to a person's success as well.

On the other hand, there can be a child of a dysfunctional family who loves God intensely, but who is poor, with bad social skills, non-athletic, carrying poverty or rejection spirits, etc. This person, although going to heaven, may live a very poor, even pathetic life of continual scarcity and other problems. In these instances, the bad or evil person lives well and the child of God lives poorly. One person is relatively happy, the other lives in continual trial and sadness.

In the case of the godly person, even though saved and going to heaven, unless he or she personally accepts God's teaching and directions and uses his or her authority to renounce the faulty inheritance and understands and uses God's tools to take God's inheritance, that person will in large part live out his or her natural physical and spiritual inheritance.

Words Move the Spirit World

The spirit world frequently functions on the basis of words. It is significant that the Bible tells us that Christ is the Word (verb – an action word). Think about it. The Bible in James 1:18 states, "Of His own will He brought us forth by the **word** of truth…." The greatest weapon you have is placing the Word of God, the words that God gives you, and the authority of God in your mouth and heart (followed by whatever actions are required).

Your mouth can **define** or **defile** your life and determine the size of the victory you'll achieve. Meditate on the following: "Look at ships; although they are large and driven by fierce winds, they are turned by a very small rudder wherever the pilot desires. Even so, the tongue is a little member and boasts great things. See how great a forest a little fire kindles! And the tongue is a fire, a world of iniquity. The tongue is so set among our members that it defiles the whole body and sets on fire the course of nature (human lives and even nature itself)…." (James 3:4–6)

Beware: What you speak will guide your actions *and* the reactions and actions of those around you in both dimensions. Your words define much of your life. Aside from the natural consequences of your words, **speaking *negatively* puts the power of faith and words in motion *against you*!** Consider carefully everything you say to God, to spirits, to yourself, and to other human beings: **Is there life in your words, or sin and death?**

Fortunately there is at least a partial remedy; when you say something that's evil, wrong, or just not useful, there is something you can do. The Bible says that none of the words of Samuel fell to the ground (I Sam 3:19). The implication of the verse is that words can fall dead and not be effective.

Cast un-useful words to the ground. Dead and cast to the ground, there is an element to them that will stop working. I have found the effect to be doubly powerful: there is freedom for others and for myself. I've personally seen the effect of doing this and I do it often by saying: "In the name of Jesus I cast to the ground as dead things the following words: _____ " (whatever I've said about something).

The passages about Samuel's words not falling to the ground explains spirit world principle. Words can fall to the ground and not have effect, all the more if we throw them to the ground with our words.

When speaking and acting on words of faith (positive faith) you must understand, believe and act. With and through faith you will understand what to say, and with and through faith you will know what to do. As a result you'll move and change what's going on in the spirit world.

More Spiritual Aspects
of Your Life

The heart

Your heart is the core of your being. It is part soul, part spirit and intimately connected to your body—in some ways it defines your essence. It needs love and, if there is a love deficit, craves it. The heart is that part of you that motivates you (along with body and soul). It is where your deepest self resides and, incidentally, it is where God resides in you. Your own heart can be your ally or your enemy.

The Bible says, "Keep your heart with all diligence; for out of it spring the issues of life." (Proverbs 4:23). Your heart can drive you to extreme actions (good and bad) and into sin. Your heart is key because it motivates you in the deepest ways. A heart for the lost can drive a person to preach, a heart for the hurting, to minister healing. A heart in need of love can drive you to seek love in God and/or in others and to activities (helpful or unhelpful, divine or depraved) to help fill the void in any way it can.

Do the very best you can to keep your heart safe. Fill it with the right things. Cravings for love can lead to relationships and sexual immorality or activities/addictions that feel good, that bring you moments of peace and momentary happiness, but which actually "war against the soul" (I Peter 2:11). Instead of healing, you'll be compelled to endure more heartbreak and yearning and distance from God. That is Satan's plan. He wants your soul. He works endlessly to damage you more every day.

Another issue with the human heart is that your mouth speaks what's inside your heart (Matthew 12:13). What comes from your mouth mixed with faith becomes a reality. That's good news *and* bad news (if your faith in God is not robust). Because of this, *it is vital to maintain your heart in right condition so you don't end up snared by your own words.*

What lies within your heart has other effects. The negative things in your heart and their resulting actions will limit you from receiving the freedom, gifts and blessings that God has for you and will also keep you from transferring them to others.

Anything that is beneficial and anything that is evil that exists in your life will (to one degree or another) manifest in results -- logical results based on spiritual laws and the principals in operation within the spirit world. Your heart is an integral part of what is in your life. Your thoughts, beliefs and actions serve to open and/or close spiritual doors and windows, for good or evil in your life, in the lives of others, and to those under your authority. The results are often difficult to predict.

Always do *the best you can.* Spend time diligently filling your heart with the Word of God and the teachings based on it; don't let them depart from your eyes or heart (Proverbs 4:20-22). Spend time in the morning reading the Bible and praying, then listen to Christian music to resist evil and realize that you do not *have to* do the ungodly things that flash through your mind like litter in a hurricane. If you think you HAVE to do something ungodly, your heart is beguiled by Satan. In some ways, the beginning of deliverance is realizing that you don't HAVE to do the tawdry things your heart craves. Even if you're addicted to something or someone, you do not *have to* indulge; but you do have to be treated for your addiction to see this truth and regain the power and authority to abandon the practice.

So, beware of what is in your heart. The Bible say in Ecclesiastes 9:3b that there is madness in it. Ask God to help you with it, to fill it with Himself and to heal it.

Spiritual bondages

God wants your heart to be filled with His love, your love for Him, faith, godly love for others, and He wants your will to be given over to desiring everything that is godly. God wants—for your sake, and because He desires a close relationship with you—for your heart to be free and healthy. Your heart, properly conditioned, will allow you to receive everything that God has for you and will free you from the devil and evil.

But when -- with your heart, the content of it, and with

your actions -- you want to please God, you won't be able to do so if unforgiveness plagues you; if you're too hurt (and not yet healed); if you have compromised yourself with the world with unholy desires or with a spirit other than the Spirit of the Lord; or if fear, doubts, or ungodly ties with other people are a part of your present game plan. To be right and do right requires a free, healthy, clean heart.

The greatness of God's creation regarding man *is choice*. Unlike animals humans have the ability to choose their courses. You are not like the ant (preprogrammed) or like a bear operating on instinct. You are not like a dog that reacts to its environment and becomes the sum of its input. **No matter what has happened to you, no matter how oppressed, you were given the power of transforming choice.** Our species alone can understand, reason, and make choices, the most important being to choose to forgive, to truly love. In this regard, you were created to be God's image-bearer, to mirror love, forgiveness, grace and to choose that which is necessary for you to be just, true, pure, and holy. (Phil 6:4.)

Forgiveness is a key heart issue and fundamental to be free of spiritual bondages. In this world there are many things, events, words and people that offend God's sensibilities and ours. Jesus is your example of how to deal with them. He came to save, heal and bless, but was crucified by those He came to help. Still, He didn't hold a grudge; to the contrary, He opened the door to forgiveness and right standing with God through His suffering.

The issue is never the offense, but how to respond to it. Because of everything God has forgiven you for, you have the obligation to forgive those who have offended you. And, to be blunt (the truth of this will set you free), you no longer have the *right* to withhold your forgiveness. Decide to forgive because Jesus forgave you; this should become the very core of your personhood.

The ability to forgive not only makes you human; the act of forgiveness is an extremely important part of the process of setting you free (and others free) and making you a warrior for God. Your lack of forgiveness is a spiritual tie (a connection to the spirit world) that binds you to life *as it was* before you knew Christ. It's old (dead) news!

To be free of the spiritual bondage of unforgiveness, begin with forgiving yourself. (Don't argue, self-forgiveness is where you *must* start—you've already lost the right to hold onto grudges, remember?). While God understands anger, unforgiveness, and justice, He reserves anger and judgment for Himself. And His anger is based on complete justice, unlike ours. Your "job" in Christ is to *forgive*; let God *repay*. Work as hard as you have to in order to surrender the offense, the resulting anger, the sense of unfairness and lack of justice. When you finally win the battle, it will transform your life.

Unforgiveness and other wrong things in your heart enrich

the soil where evil thrives in the form of spirit things and beings, and keep you bound to them. They also serve as windows, doors and connections in your heart, allowing things into your life and those you cover (family and others) and will control much of your life if you allow them in. Jesus came to give you abundant life, not life controlled directly or indirectly by evil.

Another common, major heart bondage is fear. *Fear is placing your faith in what the world or the devil says*, not in what the Bible and the Holy Spirit proclaim. *Fear is <u>negative faith</u>* which, when combined with your words and actions, <u>*brings negative results*</u>. <u>The law of faith functions in both the negative and the positive</u>. Your heart must be freed from fear. **Knowing and receiving the love of God and trusting Him in all things frees you from the bondage of fear.**

Heart ministry

I sometimes find it useful to *take an action* and to *make a proclamation.* Using unforgiveness as an example, using my hand to take action, I "take" unforgiveness with my hand as I say, "I take unforgiveness out of my heart…" As I "put" forgiveness in my heart, I say, "…and I place forgiveness there". I follow-up by saying, "I also invite you—Father, Son and Holy Spirit—to inhabit the place where unforgiveness was located." In the process, many times I've noticed that God will place additional things in my mind to act upon in the same manner. I have used the same process to remove fear, lust, pride and many other "things" from my heart.

Getting free and well is a process. It ain't easy! Without fail it will be a struggle. Just keep at it: unload the un-useful things from your heart.

Spiritual connections

The clearest example of spiritual connections is the one that joins persons who have been intimate sexually. It seems to me that these connections can also be cemented via lust (the mere *desire* to copulate with another). Affected persons are connected by "threads." Imagine invisible fiber optic connections in the spirit world. People connected in this way are in no way free, although they believe themselves to be. In reality, the connection to the other person causes both to be affected by the other. In my opinion, this is one of the reasons the apostle Paul says that immorality is a sin *against one's own body*. Immorality connects the body and spirit to another person and bonds them to some degree to what is going on in the other's existence.

Connections exist within your family and with departed ancestors, too. You should bless family members and ancestors and you should cut any ungodly ties to stop the transmission of bad habits, sin, etc. to you and your progeny.

When you accept a "favor," "healing," or any other "gift" from a spirit (good or bad), to some degree you're indebted to the spirit; you place yourself under the spirit's authority, who then becomes your "benefactor." These "gifts," even if seemingly good, come at a price and will affect your soul. The Bible says in the book of James that all good and perfect gifts come from God alone.

Worshiping a spirit and giving it offerings also forms a bond. Some churches make a serious error: they permit prayer to the spirits of dead persons (saints) and other spirits. These prayers form ties that are not permitted according to the Bible. Scriptures teach that we should pray to "our heavenly Father" as the prayer "Our Father" indicates, and that we should only worship God; no other spirit. A saved person needs to sever all ties that bind them to other spirits. (Note: Connections to spirits can be weak or almost unbreakable; the latter results in possession.)

God gave us the Bible as a guide. We should discard all traditions that have been introduced by churches that don't agree in Spirit with the Bible. The key purpose of the existence of the Bible is to know God and what He wants for and from us. He has given us an incorruptible record. <u>In the measure that we accept the Bible as the Word of God and do what it says, we find the freedom, joy, peace, health, restoration and the other good things that God has for us.</u>

The point of all this? You and I need to have our "being" in good condition: free from ungodly spiritual connections and bondages (including fear) in order to receive all that God has for us. Part of the process is to open our hearts to God, fill our hearts with good godly things, and remove all types of bonds and ties that are counterproductive and keep us in spiritual bondage.

Down the Rabbit Hole

Spirit trails

Now let's examine spirit trails. To do this, you need to think of chasing rabbits…sort of.

There are countless spirits in the spirit dimension trying to get you and me to follow them. Keep in mind, the spirit dimension is not like the earthly dimension. In the spirit world, "space" is different; for example, there was a legion of spirits in the demoniac of Gadara—so many, in fact, that they were able to fill an entire herd of pigs with their presence. The point here is that there are lots and lots spirits, whether they're inside us or not, and *they want us to follow them down their spirit trails.* I've found this useful to remember any time I'm trying to figure out which way to go.

Running with spirits down spirit trails, which way are you going to go? Here's an example of how they work: A spirit suggests a beer to you at home; sure, why not? After a couple beers, an idea comes to you; why not go to a tavern? It isn't as lonely there. You know that at the tavern people are talking, drinking, watching a game, having a good time. At the same time, the suggesting spirit knows that the tavern hosts a good number of alcoholic, lust, and drug spirits and the people who willingly follow them down their spirit holes. Their suggestions are seductive...*come away with me...have another drink...forget your troubles for a while...."*

You go. Thoughts enter your head when an attractive customer bends over the pool table. Your eyes fixate. Another beer goes down. You go down the spirit's thought path. Lust spirits make a suggestion; your body reacts. Your target's lust spirit makes sure he or she responds.

Don't give up!

You're running down a spirit trail--and it's **not** the Holy Spirit's. You've followed the spirits into their lair, into their strongholds. Hordes of spirits are seducing you....

Red alert! Divert!

The Holy Spirit prompts you to leave...but you take another look and join a pool game. The game finishes. You go out to join your new "friend" for a smoke, and the marijuana comes out…oh, what the heck, one toke. Resistance softens. You exchange a kiss. The spirits flood your mind with ideas … and more spirit trails present themselves. How far are you going to go? Who will prevail?

A more subtle example is anger. You are content and then something happens that disturbs you. Thought of past offenses enter your mind. You fixate on them. Soon you're upset. The anger may just destroy your day, but perhaps you make a phone call to the offender. The anger grows, plans are made: a physical visit, perhaps a lawsuit. You are on another spirit path led by an evil spirit.

Be aware of your environment. Identify what's happening on the physical and spirit levels; how are the spirits working? Your unseen saboteurs are real "persons," that is, spirits made of spirit material, and they have a plan for your life. Watch out for them! Recognize how they work. Don't follow them. Look for and follow God's leading.

Weavings

What you say, do, and are connected to -- weaves "a tapestry" in the spirit world. Remember: just as things are woven in the physical, the same action exists in the spirit world. Evil wants to lock you into the threads that he weaves and that he gets you to weave. You get locked, or sewn, into a reality (life). Know and understand what is happening in the invisible world, fight to undo what evil has woven, and do and say what is required to weave your life into, and with what, God has for you. In Jesus we have authority to undo our own weavings and the weavings of evil.

Communications From the Spirit World

God speaks to your mind via word thoughts and words. He communicates directly to your heart by depositing things there. He also communicates with your emotions.

But understand this: Satan also communicates in the form of thoughts. Satan *imposes* his thoughts on unsuspecting minds, suggesting things he wants you to do or at least consider doing. He is constantly trying to mold you into who he wants you to be, and to transform your life according to his plan. He also deposits things into your heart and emotions.

Basic thoughts Satan will impose are often in the form of "I." "I want…" "I need…" "I would like…" I think…" He puts these suggestions inside your mind so you'll assume it's your own thought, but he isn't limited to just this tactic; far from it. **He often directly tells people what to do.** The majority of your thoughts aren't generated by you; they come from a spirit, either an evil spirit, one of God's angels, or directly from God.

From the moment you meet Jesus, you become engaged in a spiritual battle to discern whether the communications you receive are from God and His compatriots or from the devil and his minions. Although God is working directly in your heart and spirit (as does Satan) to mold them from outside the mental process, your mind is still a key player, so it's useful to learn to discern and distinguish the voice of God from the voice of the devils (all spirits not submitted to God the Father, Son and Holy Spirit).

The voice of God is often described as a still small voice (inside the mind). It speaks to your understanding. But Satan speaks to your understanding, too, and can even mimic God's "voice". Many times I've seen believers think that God is speaking when in fact it is an evil spirit. In many churches in countries of intense spiritual opening, half or more of the congregation act on instructions given by a deceiving spirit claiming to be the Holy Spirit. This misinterpretation is also common in the United States.

I don't know of any better way to learn how to hear the voice of God other than to listen and discern the author of whatever enters your heart and mind. But listening to what the spirits say should NEVER supplant reading the Bible. The Bible is God's written word. It is error-free and explains who he is and how to know Him. My experience is that when God wants to communicate with me *directly,* He most often "points out" portions of the Bible as I'm reading it, or gives new or specific meaning to verses or portions of passages as my eyes and spirit encounter them. Much of this book was written through this process.

When you do recognize spirit thoughts or "hear" spirits, the Bible will serve to help you determine if what you're hearing is from God. ***What you receive or "hear" from the spirit realm must coincide with the written Word.*** But beware! At times evil spirits will be able to highlight or direct you to a section of the Bible to mislead you or (more often) to condemn (as opposed to convict) you, so even if you believe you have clear direction or insight from God and the Bible, if numerous people of God tell you "No, your conclusion or direction is wrong," ***believe them***. You have been deceived as to the source of your information.

In a men's shelter, I met a fellow who had quit his job just two months before his retirement date and lost his family, believing that God was directing him to do so. The leadership and pastors of at least two churches had told him that he was not following God but, in his pride, he was convinced he was hearing God and that they were deaf to God's confirmation of his actions.

Satan and the spirits that follow him also speak through religious prophets and through those who "channel" the "words" spirits. Jeremiah 2:8b reports, "The prophets prophesied by

Baal." All religions and systems have their "prophets" preaching, teaching, and proclaiming the doctrines placed in their mind and hearts. The *system* is the same; the *spirit information source* is what changes.

Your mind is a dynamic thing, continually analyzing, sorting, weighing and considering ideas and actions. *Whatever enters it*—especially if it's more carefully scrutinized and not instantly discarded—*affects you.* The continuous onslaught of communications from the world of evil spirits is dangerous. Peter, in his first letter, verse 13, shows a deep insight into the nature of the human mind; heavy stuff for a man who started out as an uneducated young fisherman! He warns us to "gird up the loins of your mind." My understanding of this passage is that we are to protect our prolific minds and be watchful, keeping them at full potential– undamaged, prepared, abstaining and wise. In other words, protect yourself! (Put on your mental jock strap or iron maiden.)

Vibes and emanations

Aside from thought and word communications, certain spirits emit their nature (others can mask their nature and emit a lie). For example, lust spirits make you feel lustful just by their being near you. Similarly, ruling spirits of the air over an area affect what you want and how you think and feel while in their territory. For example, when my family lived in Mexico we could live without a desire to spend money. When we crossed the border into the U.S., a half mile into the U.S. we wanted to go to a mall and shop, even though the thought and desire were non-existent just minutes before in Mexico. The ruling spirits communicated the desire to us and exerted control through it. I have noted the effect of ruling spirits even over sections of a town, or between towns. Desires and thoughts that can touch our whole being come from the spiritual rulers over those areas.

Visual and other communications

Before the word "prophet" was coined, the term "seer" was often used. A seer or prophet is someone who can see into the spirit world, in the sense of seeing what God wants us to see, including our future. (2 Kings 6:16 –19.) It is still entirely possible to see into the spirit world. Fasting and spending lots of time reading the Bible nourishes your spirit and helps you see in the prophetic sense.

I have seen the Kingdom of God personally. It is indeed "the jewel of great beauty" as described in the book of Revelation 21. I have seen Jesus and also the human spirits within the bodies of people. Equally as useful are the things that God has shown me so that I can effectively minister to people in the area of their needs. Fasting and the amount of time I spent reading and understanding the Bible helped me "see" into the spirit area.

Through witchcraft a person can also see into the spirit world. The only other person I have encountered who could see the human spirit person inside human physical bodies was an ex-witch. But conscious entry into the spirit world through witchcraft is perilous; it requires opening yourself to deceiving (evil) spirits. In the process, the heart and spirit are fused to them. Any pleasantness on the part of deceiving spirits is a ruse; they are evil.

How Satan communicates in the physical realm

Aside from communicating with you directly (through other spirits that have left the True God or via occasional audible voices) the devil also teaches his systems and ways through newspapers, magazines, radio, television, human beings controlled by him, and the culture we live in. Even Christian believers, by acting in accordance with human nature, speak and act according to the will of the devil. Notice that God has commanded us to love Him with every part of us (heart, soul, body and spirit) so we're completely tied to him and can speak His words and manifest His love. The physical world belongs to Satan; humankind ***deeded it to him*** through sin and rebellion.

Communication confusion

Our God is not confused, nor is he the god of confusion. Confusion is the evil one's tactic to keep God's people from identifying communications from God and knowing/doing what is good for us (and/or others) as we accomplish His will. Confusion is also what Satan and his minions use to keep people who do not know Jesus from coming to know Him and from doing what is right.

For God's people seeking a direct answer, one of the common tactics is to offer an excess of information. Rather than receive a simple answer from God, there are multiple possibilities, perceptions, and even "signs." For those who are seeking a mental "impression" (a "voice"), there are many impressions and voices that all "sound like" the voice of God.

Another common tactic is for Satan to place a wall of mental "static" between you and God's voice, so that nothing you hear is clear; you discern only static. Sin and condemnation act as walls between your spirit and soul and God. All you'll "hear" this way is absence or condemnation.

Fasting helps clear the confusion, identify the various voices, break through the static, and reduce or eliminate the condemnation, but it usually doesn't happen immediately. <u>Fasting is a very effective tool. (More on this later.)</u>

A wonderful example of Satan's effort to keep mankind from hearing from God is in the book of Daniel 10:12 & 13. Daniel fasted to hear God and God dispatched the Archangel Michael with a message. **Michael had to fight 40 days to get through. Satan's ways of blocking God's messages vary, but the purpose is the same.**

God's messages aren't contradictory, they are consistent. Their purpose is in keeping with what the Bible says. But when trying to discern His "voice," there will be confusion; Satan will make sure of that! When in doubt, do what the Bible says: Love God, your neighbor and yourself and keep steer clear of sin and sinful thoughts.

Spiritual Life

Spiritual life is not the same as spiritual existence. As mentioned earlier, all spirits have eternal existence *but only those connected to God have life*. Life is not existence, life is being connected to God (us in Him and Him in us) (John 14:21 & 23, John 17:3). Life is God himself who flows through us, restores us, heals us and blesses us.

Satan has already been judged and sentenced; he cannot repent. He does not have and cannot attain life. He is a dead spirit in eternal deterioration. Everything of his kingdoms is technically dead and produces death because they are not connected, and cannot connect, with God. All religions and witchcraft in their various forms open access to the spirit dimension, but are not life. Conscious access to the spirit dimension is nothing more than conscious access. Seeing, hearing and talking to spirits comes either through seeking access, because of the lack of covering, or generational indwelling spirits.

Death: The Systems of The Devil and of This World

- Satan's various religions, kingdoms, and other systems are planned and used against you. Their focus is to **rob, destroy and kill. (John 10:10)**. Each kingdom and system is for the purpose of keeping us from knowing the true God: Jesus who came in the flesh to manifest God and *save* us. In the matter of religions, *Satan captures people so they worship a ruling spirit that is not God.*

- All of this world's methods, religions, philosophies, and systems involve spirits and spiritual interaction.

- The operating systems (all based on thoughts, philosophies, teachings, religions, and satisfaction of needs and desire) of this world are under the authority of Satan. The Bible says he is the prince of this world (ruler).

- There are countless spiritual systems, religions, philosophies, etc., under Satan's authority.

- All that belongs to and comes from Satan is death; death that can be seen, or disguised death.

- Satan's spiritual kingdoms (religions, witchcraft, etc.) are systems the devil created.

- Satan is the father of lies; he does everything possible

to conceal his purpose. He offers counterfeit life and counterfeit freedom.

- The systems of this world that the devil gives you to navigate life in order to get what you want, including social interaction, ultimately are based on selfishness: using power, vengeance, struggle, taking and killing with body and words (look what the kids do through cyber bullying).

- The rule of this world is one of immorality, lack of ethics, and other sins that bind us to death and spirits through spiritual bondages derived from lust, misplaced allegiance, and wrongdoing (not necessarily our own).

- The devil uses the "favors" that you receive from spirits that "help you" as traps so he can make you his possession, so you're bound to him rather than to God and Life.

- The religions, philosophies, wisdoms and systems of this world are being preached and taught on every side, using the people and media (mostly unconsciously) controlled by the devil.

- Satan operates based on natural and spiritual laws. He is not God and cannot change God's laws. He cannot escape from the laws, nor can he attain grace through Christ's death; he has already been judged and sentenced.

- The good and the beautiful that is seen in human beings and the world come from God. (Note: the goodness of God is manifested by the marvelous bodies he gave us and through the wonderful planet he created for us to inhabit. *We and creation itself have become insane through sin and the kingship of evil.*)

- Everything Satan has created is for the purpose of keeping you away from Jesus so that he can destroy your life and keep you spiritually dead until he can at last claim your physical life.

A quick additional point: we are not evolving into something better. God did not create a mess that we and nature are trying to change into something good. God created something good that we invited the devil into. As a result, even our bodies and human nature are no longer "good". We live in a body that desires what is not good for it or our spirit and soul with a nature that so quickly can default to doing what is wrong. So it is not only the devil and devils that work against us, but our own beings desire wrong.

In the next section you'll learn more—much more—about your Savior. Your campaign against devils and demons **must** have Christ Jesus at its foundation or your protracted battles against evil—no matter how skillfully fought—will be doomed to failure.

"For I am persuaded that neither death nor life,
nor angels nor principalities (ruling spirits) nor powers
(devils), nor things present nor things to come... shall
be able to separate us from the love of God which
is in Christ Jesus our Lord." Romans 8:38

The Script:
Into The Game to Fix It

There is a real God

I practice law. I deal with evidence, part of which is testimony. If there are ten people who testify to a murder, even without a body, there will be a conviction. All religions, witches, warlocks, and spiritualists testify as to a spirit world, spirits, and some God or gods. To say there is no God requires complete rejection of their testimony! You simply can't get there and be intellectually honest. The only real question is, "Who is God?"

Who is Jesus?

Jesus is the second person of the Triune (three in One)

God. All three co-inhabit and co-occupy all of existence inside and **outside** of time and space; they have co-existed forever; they are of the same substance (spirit); have the same purposes, thoughts, desires and *heart*. There is no division and there never has been any division or separation between them (except perhaps at the cross when Jesus became sin for us); they are all completely and equally good, holy, kind, just, and all powerful (within the limits and systems that the three-person God alone has set). The unity of material (spirit and eternal Life), space and existence (all together everywhere), and person (they are the same in nature, heart and purpose), is why they are One. There is only One God in three persons. When you know Jesus, you know the Father and the Holy Spirit. In John 14:9b & 10, Jesus said: "…he who has seen Me has seen the Father, so how can you say, 'Show us the Father?' Do you not believe that I am in the Father, and the Father in Me?" Paul in Colossians 1:15–16 says: "He is the image of the invisible God…for by Him all things were created that are in heaven and earth, visible and invisible…." The prophet Isaiah, *centuries before* the birth of Jesus, spoke of Jesus as follows: "For unto us a child is born, unto us a Son is given…and his name will be called Wonderful, Counselor, Mighty God, Everlasting Father, Prince of Peace…." (Isaiah 9:6)

His acts while on earth and His continued acts in our lives show He is God. (More of this to come.)

The Why of Everything Relevant to Jesus

It makes a good movie: God came into His own creation in a human body to rescue it for the purpose of freeing us from the power of darkness and to take us into His kingdom (Col. 1:13). To do so, He had to do some things in time and space (here on earth) and in the spirit world (we will see what later). In His time on earth he proved Himself to be God through miracles, signs and wonders manifesting power over heaven, earth and death.

Where did he come from?

Heaven. It is real. It is the diverse spirit dimension. God the Father lives there (and has most of it blocked off from evil). Jesus came from there and went back: John 16:28 and 33, "I came from the Father and have come into the world. Again, I leave the world and go to the Father." It is the place from which Jesus' rule emanates: John 18:36, "My kingdom is not of this world…."

Heaven is the place to go to – Earth is only temporary.

Through Christ Jesus, it is **the** destination and your real home. Your true citizenship resides there (Phil. 3:20).

Don't get too comfortable and keep your bags packed: You and I are merely pilgrims here on earth (I Peter 1:1). We are just traveling through on our way somewhere else (heavenly dimension).

Contrary to some ideologues, Heaven is not an "opiate of the masses," something ministers preach to soothe us so we live our lives here as victims. This book is about living the abundant life that God says He has for us while here on earth; but note this earth is corrupted and things can be awful in spite of God's provision.

Insanity

Because of humankind's **insane** choice to become independent and the fact that we live in a fallen body that craves sin in an environment that subjects us to the continual influence of evil, life here will never and can never be **completely** good.

In worst case scenarios, life here on earth becomes pure trauma. In those cases, we can take solace in our future world, heaven. We don't have to endure this world forever and, thank God, we don't have to be reincarnated to earn salvation which due to our fallen nature (let's be honest) we could never earn.

How to get to heaven

"I am the truth, the **way** and the life," said Jesus. You have to connect with God through Jesus to be allowed into heaven. He's there (in that very real place) waiting for us and making a place for us.

Jesus said:

John 13:36, "Where I am going you cannot follow me now [while alive in the body], but you shall follow me [later]...."

John 14: 2 and 3, "In my Father's house are many mansions, if it were not so, I would have told you. I go to prepare a place for you, I will come again and receive you to Myself; that where I am, there you may be also."

What will heaven be like?

True heaven (the spirit world where the devil is not, but God is) will truly be the manifested Kingdom of God: no operating system errors, no glitches, no problems. Everyone and everything in it will be connected to God and will exist according to God's original plan. There will be no death, no pain, no hurt, no conflict, no trauma; just joy, peace, happiness and unity. Everything will run according to the plan and purpose of God. Everyone and everything will have its proper place and be contented in and with it. You and I will be exactly who God created us to be and we'll fulfill our purpose in peace and joy. Perhaps it's worth mentioning that at some point and in some way, heavenly life will also have a physical component. A very cool and hip new place without the flaws that man made by messing with the operating system's rules.

The Promised Abundant Life While Here on Earth

The abundant life that the Bible promises you is not only the full meal deal in heaven, but for here too. It will be easy in heaven; here, we have to work hard to get it. The so-called "good life" (as defined by society) is not the abundant life God wants to give you.

God the Father through Jesus' sacrifice wants to give you a *truly* good life: fellowship with Himself, *love*, **peace**, joy, freedom from the fear of death, financial provision, acceptance, friends and yourself. As you serve Him, He offers you *your* true self.

The reality is that the roles, identities, activities, and attitudes that you and I have accepted—the mindless or one-dimensional life, the endless search for love, the drinking, drugs, sex, power, money, endless adventure, etc.—all are errant attempts to find a good and abundant life. We live lives of sin trying to find peace, pleasure, and all the rest. Through faith and trusting God, He gives us the focus and relationship to delete the unnecessary and un-useful stuff (roles, un-useful activities, improper sex, drinking, escape, etc.) and gives us what those things often promise *but cannot deliver*. In God, and through God, we lose the sin and its ultimate destructiveness and get God and get what He has for us here.

The Kingdom of God

The Kingdom (rule, way and system) of God is based upon love and forgiveness. It is comprised of love, compassion, forgiveness, blessing, and provision. Through and in His government, He gives us authority and victory over the fallen world, fallen creation, and the devil. God's kingdom is a government of wellness.

We receive the full benefits of the Kingdom of God through the cross of Jesus Christ. There is no other way to reach and know God and receive all of His blessings (physical and spiritual benefits). Because of sin the human race died. All are dead, i.e. separated from God. Christ died saddled with our sins, illnesses and pains **to remove death and its effects;** He also paid the complete penalty for not obeying the law. The kingdom of God is for all who have surrendered themselves to God by entering through the door (Jesus) that He opened.

Christ died to destroy death. He resurrected to give us life. Death to death, life to Life. (2 Cor. 2:16). God's kingdom is life, good things (spiritual and physical), provision and victory.

Christ is the only door through which we have victory over this world's systems and Satan's way of doing things. Because of the cross, we can leap from death to life. We enter as sinners and condemned (separated from God); we come out forgiven and free. We enter sick and emerge with the power and authority to be healthy and whole. We enter filled with sin and come out clean and being filled with God. We enter under the devil's authority and come out a conqueror over the devil, his ways of doing things, and the garbage that he has put in our lives.

The cross is the point of forgiveness, removal of sin and the stain of sin, and of power. It is where we get united with God, and through Christ's death on it have access to the blessings, answers and the help that all human beings desire. If we follow Christ in and with faith, we have access to all the blessings of His kingdom.

Satan is on the other side of the cross. Because he is evil he is sentenced and bound from the cross, *so he hates the cross and grace. He hates God and he hates us even more because <u>we have the option</u> to go through the cross to life, leaving death and the dead behind; <u>he doesn't</u>.* There is nothing good, interesting, kind or noble in or about the devil: he is simply evil, out to destroy God's creation—you and everything and everyone he can get his hands on.

This promised new life, with authority over the devil and his ways, belongs to you if and when you elect to take it and begin to fight to leave behind the ungodly parts of your human nature, your inherited life, your "own" life, and the world with its bondages and ties that imprison you.

The issue is not <u>whether</u> God can do or bless, the issue is will you receive what God freely offers? To receive the fullness of God's blessings, you must be willing to change and become the new person that God wants you to be: ***someone who can receive, keep and live the blessings of God.*** This requires work. The Bible says that our work is to believe in the Lord Jesus Christ, not just believe *in* Jesus but *to believe in all He said and did.*

At the moment you allow Jesus into your heart, you win the victory over death (because you have eternal life). 1 John 4:4 says, "You are of God, little children, and have overcome them, because He who is in you is greater that he who is in the world." As long as you stay with God, you maintain that victory, but the rest of the victory will be life-long in achieving; in fact, upon conversion, your battle against evil intensifies. (Satan doesn't like to lose; it infuriates him, so he makes big plans to destroy your resolve, to derail your effectiveness, and destroy your faith.)

Purpose

Most of us have commented on our seeming lack of purpose at one time or another. Certainly for those who believe in the non-existence of a good God, there is no point to life; existence is frequently viewed as a cosmic joke or a series of colossal evolutionary mishaps. Oh, life may have purpose and meaning during certain times—as when raising a family for example—but beyond immediate needs, there seems to be no purpose for folks who have no relationship to Christ. Taking care of the planet, caring for animals, etc. often offers a sense of purpose, but there is no **overall purpose** … outside of God. After all, if there is no eternal purpose, there is no *real* purpose, only what you decide is purposeful.

In Christ, we come to understand our place in creation and purpose. At a future time, in Christ, all of creation will regain its purpose. Originally, God intended physical creation to be a perfect place to live for a creation perfectly submitted to God. All creation was to co-exist in unity, love, and meaning with the purpose being **to know and serve God by loving and honoring all that He has made and all that He is**. Knowing God, the quintessential template of physical and spiritual life, starts the process of giving meaning to everything. Being with Him then and now, fully in His presence and doing what He says, was *and is* absolute fulfillment. With Him, we become who He created us to be for the purposes He intended. Outside of Him, there is not and never can be true purpose.

Your purpose, therefore, is to know God (the true and only real God), to spend time with Him, and to serve Him. The immediate service He wants is for you to fellowship with Him, learn from Him and fight for yourself, your family, loved ones and all of this creation. He wants you to do what is necessary to fight evil, to act and love with Jesus' power in His name, and free yourself and others from evil. You have immediate purpose and future purpose. The absolute truth and reality is that in Christ you are a very important resource to God and warrior for God. You are a fully armed, formerly impotent hobbit like creature, now powerful against evil.

Don't get lost in what I am saying, you do not give up the daily tasks of life, but that you incorporate your spiritual life in Jesus into your daily life for yourself, your family and for others.

As you go forward in God, He will do wonderful things in your life and in the lives of others. Know God, follow Him, and do what He says.

A Bible passage to light your way:

"...I, the LORD, will hear them; I, the God of Israel, will not forsake them. I will open rivers in desolate heights, and fountains in the midst of the valleys; I will make the wilderness a pool of water, and the dry land springs of water. I will plant in the wilderness the cedar and the acacia tree, the myrtle and the oil tree; I will set in the desert the cypress tree and the pine and the box tree together...." Isaiah 41:17–19.

What God is saying here is that He wants desert hills and dry lands to spring to life; He wants the arid parts of our lives to rebound, to become lush and robust – that is God's work, but we have a part to get what God has for us.

Free Will

It's ultimately up to you to decide how much of God and His inheritance (gift to us through Jesus' death), life and reality you want. Every aspect of it is available, but most people don't even choose cost-free, simple salvation! Many children of God don't want to work for more or battle demons to achieve victories; they accept what God offers easily... but it is a ***mere fraction*** of their actual inheritance. Others want more, but haven't been taught what Jesus did for them and how to get it.

The Bible says you can reign in life *together* with Jesus Christ. It's your decision to take up the scepter and reign or not.

To reign in your life (rather than the devils reigning) takes will, effort, *constancy,* work and sacrifice. When you don't see results every time, or when you fall in a little or big way, great faith and trust are required to keep doing right, choosing right, defending and fighting – doing the things you need to do for yourself, your family, other believers, and the world.

Focus especially on your family and those you minister to; they need your protection. In some areas, or with some people, a time will come when your work is done, the protection or healing complete. At that time, a change will be required in your defense and/or offense strategy according to God's leading but the principles you learn here will always apply.

How to know what choices to make

Fix your mind on God and the truth that God alone offers you a truly good and abundant life. Understand the battle and the weapons used against you and the weapons you have (2 Cor. 10:3 & 4). You are blind to the spirit realm and fight until you understand the unseen; how it works and how you address it. You learn what to do from the Bible and Holy Spirit-led teaching. As you read along in this book, I'll be throwing spotlights on various godly tried-and-true strategies.

God wants to give you spiritual gifts that will give you spiritual eyes, ears, and weapons. It may be that the spiritual gifts referred to in I Corinthians chapters 12, 13, & 14 exist to endow you with spiritual senses. The baptism of the Holy Spirit is an additional degree and special manifestation of the Holy Spirit. *When gifts that come through the baptism and infilling of the Holy Spirit are fully functioning, the people of God are an effective offensive and defensive fighting unit.* Since Life/life is much governed by Holy Spirit power vs. unclean spirit power, the battle of darkness is to limit the Holy Spirit's influence over you as much as possible.

Through understanding your true environment, the authority you have in Christ Jesus and your decision to act (exercise your will in alignment with God's will) you throw a monkey wrench to interrupt Satan's plans. And much of what he achieves, you can **undo** through the power of the cross, your spiritual inheritance, spiritual gifts, and the great power of God that He uses to benefit you.

A clarification: when I mention **power and authority**, I do not mean the power or authority acquired by "spiritual secrets" or occult practices or by seeking favor with evil spirits or through witchcraft. On the contrary, the power, weapons and knowledge of God are given by God to His children and **revealed for all to see in the Holy Bible**. They are for each and every member of His family, subject only to our decision to use them. The battle is His; he wants to equip you for the fight. He guides you and moves you, but you have to respond and do your part.

Even though there are many dangers—sin, vulnerability, evil spirits, mistakes, discouragement, and our hearts going astray—through what Jesus Christ did for you, you are more than a conqueror if you continue in Him to grow and do what's necessary.

The Bible Teaches That in Christ We are the Following:

1. We are sons of God; He is joined to us with His love, life and power flowing in us.
2. We have a new nature.
3. The *love* of sinful pleasure has died within us.
4. **We are loved.**
5. We are co-heirs with Christ; God wants us to have the victory that Christ enjoyed.
6. In Christ the spirits are subject to us.
7. In Christ we have power over all of Satan's power.
8. In Christ we have authority and power over all of Satan's work, including sicknesses and pain.
9. We are beneficiaries of the blessings of God.
10. We are a new creation!!!!!!

The key to receiving what God has for you is to act in faith **with** faith.

Victorious and empowered in God

Psalm 144, says:

"Blessed be the Lord my Rock,

Who trains my hands for war,

And my fingers for battle."

Psalm 146, verses 7b and 8 states:

"The Lord gives freedom to the prisoners.

The Lord opens the eyes of the blind;

The Lord raises those who are bowed down...."

The Bible says that God is "My fortress, my high tower and my deliverer, my shield and the One in whom I take refuge." Psalm 144:2

Your part is to learn, act, and take the victory, giving praise and thanks to the Lord.

Psalm 145

"I will extol You, my God, O King; And I will bless Your name forever and ever."

Will of God

God's will is:

1. To be in relationship with his creation.
2. To share friendship with you.
3. To love.

4. To bless (give good things).

5. To give freedom.

6. To make you *yourself* (who you really are – not a ruse or a fantasy person).

7. To heal

8. To help/save

9. To defeat all His (and therefore your) enemies.

10. To give you an abundant life.

Through focusing on God, the things of God and **faith** you can move forward and receive God's will for your life. The Palmist says in Psalm 141:10 – "Let the wicked fall into their own nets while I <u>escape safely</u>."

The will of God is to help in a genuine and personal form. If you sincerely want God and what He has given you and are in right standing with God through Christ, then the victory is yours.

God, through the voice of His prophet Isaiah, says in chapter 41 verses 10–13: "Fear thou not; for I am with thee: be not dismayed; for I am thy God: I will *strengthen* thee; yea, I will *help* thee; yea, I will *uphold* thee with the right hand of my righteousness. *Behold, all they that were incensed against thee shall be ashamed and confounded*: they shall be as nothing; and they that strive with thee shall perish. Thou shalt seek them, and shalt not find them, even them that contended with thee: they that war against thee shall be as nothing, and as a thing of nought. For I the Lord thy God will hold thy right hand, saying unto thee, *Fear not; I will help thee." (KJ)*

To receive all that God has for you, it's essential to go with Him 100% as He leads. This will take a lot of "releasing" the persona you turned yourself into during all the before-Christ years while you were so busy protecting yourself in the only ways you knew how. **It is not easy.**

Our God is the Real God

Isaiah 44:6 God says: "I am the first, and I am the last; and <u>beside me there is no God.</u>"

...and powerful:

God says: "Is my hand shortened at all that it cannot redeem? Or have I no power to deliver? Indeed with My rebuke I dry up the sea, I make the rivers a wilderness: their fish stink because there is no water, and die of thirst." (Isaiah 50:2b.)

Isaiah 51:3: "For the Lord will comfort Zion, He will comfort all her waste places; <u>He will make her wilderness like Eden, And her desert like the garden of the Lord; Joy and gladness will be found in it, Thanksgiving and the voice of melody.</u>"

God works through His Word. His Word *is* **power** and *has* **power.** Genesis 1:1 and 3 "In the beginning God created the heavens and the earth...then God <u>said</u> 'let there be light' and there was light." Note: John 1:14, Jesus is the Word (verb) of God; everything was made through Him. He is God's Son.

Even though you often can't know or understand what God is doing, or whether He's hearing you, if your heart is directed toward Him, be assured that He *is* responding. He knows what He's doing. You have to put in 100% effort (remember: you live under free will) if you want to receive what God wants you to have. You also have to *let go* of your ties with the world, evil, spirits, and <u>even with parts of your own soul</u> to reach and take what God has for you.

God responds. When the prophet called out to God in I Kings 18:37–38, saying "Hear me, O Lord, hear me that this people may know that You are the Lord God, and that You have turned their hearts back to you again. <u>Then the fire of the Lord fell and consumed the burnt sacrifice, and the wood and the stones and the dust, and it licked up the water that was in the trench.</u>"

When you cry out to Jesus to help you, to save your life, and accept Him into your heart, He comes to live inside of you. He begins influencing your will, what you think, what you do, what you pray, what you want. God responds every moment to your greatest need, which is… (drum roll, please…) …God. (If this surprises you, you're not quite there yet.)

In my opinion, God's agreement to live inside you (to give you victory over all His enemies) is a greater response than the fire falling from the sky mentioned in the last paragraph. And God wants more for you, but you have to understand how to get it. (I'm providing knowledge and the tools you'll need in this book.) You also have to spend time with Him and do things that will strengthen your spirit so you can hang with Him, through thick and thin, in perfect shalom (peace).

The Cross: What It's About and Why

The work that Christ did on the cross at Calvary is the basis of your relationship with God and reveals His love for you. The cross is what allows God, in his holiness, to live in you and you in Him. Through the work of the cross, God's love and nature (life, compassion, health and blessings) flow to and within you and the rest of His redeemed.

Death, sickness and problems exist because of sin. Sadly, right now this world reflects more of the work of Satan than of God because humans have chosen the devil's rabbit trails and holes. The entire physical world system has gone insane. Choosing the devil is to accept and behave according to his systems, doing what he says, even without necessarily consciously making a deal or surrendering to him. Choosing for the devil is choosing the path of self will and **independence** (separation) from God. Note, however, that the person in this position may not understand that this is his/her situation. In fact, the person may believe he/she is serving God, because he/she does not know the real God.

God performed seven essential tasks to allow Him to be able to give all His blessings to you and for you to be able to receive them.

1. Christ took away your sin. You are no longer loaded with sin. God is able to have relationship with you (and live inside you and you in Him) as a consequence of your being sinless in Jesus Christ. God is Holy and does not accept sin in His presence.

2. God the Son took your punishment. He was your substitute. Because of what Jesus did, you no longer deserve to be punished; neither are you guilty. Because in Christ Jesus you no long merit punishment, God can *justly* bless and help you. The nature of God is love, but He is also just. His justice obligates Him to punish the guilty.

3. Christ carried your sins and infirmities to hell. Hell is the garbage dump of the universe. As mentioned, there are spirit things. Sin, curses, infirmities, etc. have existence as spirit things. God had to send someone to take those things away, to free you and me from them. No one, aside from God, has the power to do this, which is another

reason God the Son came to earth. (Remember: the spirit world is both logical and real and deals with all matters in a logical and real way).

4.   God freed you from the law and the curse for not obeying it. The curses are written in the book of Deuteronomy, chapter 28, verses 15–22. The curse includes illnesses, pain, grief, poverty, etc. The curse and its parts are punishment for not doing what is right.

5.   God mortally wounded your natural desire to sin and your enjoyment of sin.

6.   God gave you a new nature.

7.   God gave you the ultimate Spirit power by putting Christ inside you.

Key verses of the Bible dealing with the work of the cross mentioned above are:

I Peter 2:24: "Who Himself bore our sins in His own body on the tree, that we, having died to sins, might live for righteousness - by whose stripes you were healed."

Isaiah 53:4 & 5 (NIV) "Surely He took up our infirmities and carried our sorrows; Yet we esteemed him stricken by God, smitten by him, and afflicted. But He was pierced for our transgressions, he was crushed for our iniquities; the punishment that brought us peace was upon him, and by his wounds we are healed."

Romans 6:6: "…our old man was crucified with Him, that the body of sin might be done away with, that we should no longer be slaves to sin."

Galatians 3:13 (NIV): "Christ redeemed us from the curse of the law by becoming a curse for us, for it is written: 'Cursed is everyone who is hung on a tree.'"

2 Corinthians 5:17 (Good New Bible): "When anyone is joined to Christ he is a new being…."

Colossians 1:17 (Good News Bible): "…Christ is in you…."

Through the work of the cross and by your acceptance of Jesus Christ as savior, God is by your side and inside you. He acts to bless you with His help in every part of your being and existence. The issue is whether you are willing to receive what God has for you.

God is not mean. God is love!!!!!!

The specific provisions of forgiveness, blessings, and salvation for those in Christ do not apply to those outside Jesus. Without forgiveness through the cross, it is impossible to *know* God. An unconverted person remains mostly separated from God as a result of the Fall of Adam and Eve. Without Christ, without the cross, no one can have an *intimate relationship* with the true God, nor can we please God because of our fallen nature.

God's heart for all his "descendants"

Please understand one thing clearly: Every person on this planet is a "descendant" of God, but not all of them are His children. He has given each of us free will; He created and only *directs* our human spirit, He does not "OWN" them or we'd be robots without the ability to say "No, thanks." Without our spirits, our bodies are dead. God is reaching out to **everyone** of every faith and condition to establish an intimate family relationship through Jesus. The tragedy is that not many accept the invitation.

People outside of Jesus are like children born of a sexual encounter between a man and woman. The child does not *personally* know his or her father. When the child reaches adulthood, if a relationship is not established, the child remains merely a descendant, not a son or a daughter. The child may understand that Mr. _____ is his or her father just as a person may know that there is a God, but he or she may elect never to connect with him.

God the Father's heart is to bless, help, heal, and love. He does everything possible to establish a Daddy relationship (which **the child, not the Father,** rejects) with each person. That is, God works on behalf of all his descendants to help them and He holds open the door of establishing a Daddy relationship with his children through Jesus. He is Daddy to those who want to be His kids *and* who enter through the door He has provided. God through Jesus Christ is reaching to mankind. Religion is only man's testimony of an encounter with the spirit world, spirits and their teachings.

This explains part of God's motivation in allowing His kids to suffer at the hands of His descendants. He is patient and showing His goodness even on those who persecute His kids because the persecutors also are His "descendants." God is reaching out to all; His heart is that they will choose to reach back to Him and elect to enter His family.

God's Nature and Character

The greatest thing that God has for you is Himself. From Him, from His nature, flows everything you require: love, life, salvation, understanding, knowledge and all of His blessings. At His death on the cross, Christ gave you, as your inheritance, oneness with God, so you can have God and enjoy the things that come from Him, from his nature and Being. **God is life.**

When Moses asked God His name, He defined Himself as "I AM" (Exodus 3:14). In various other parts of the Bible He elaborates, saying He is the Living God. In Genesis, the Bible says He created all things, including all living creatures. He is both alive and gives life. Life is part of His nature, Who He is; life comes from Him. His life becomes yours when you accept Jesus as your savior. Through your acceptance of Jesus you connect directly to God the Father, God the Son and God the Holy Spirit which results in the flow of Life to you. In John 11:25, Jesus says, "I am the resurrection and the life…"

The message of the cross is the message of life. It is life to life and death to death (2 Cor. 2:16). It is the way out of the kingdom of death and the way out of Satan, the prince of death. Satan hates the cross and detests the idea that you should come to know what comes to you through Jesus' death on it.

Connected to the Source of life, you have access to life and health. God Himself flows to you. God's presence and provision result in healing. Jesus' death specifically made a provision for your healing, allowing you to reconnect to God and through His suffering remove your pain and infirmities.

God is love

The Bible tells us that God is love (I John 4:8). The Bible also tells us that love is of God (I John 4:7).

Christ Himself is God (John 1:1). And to repeat what I wrote earlier, in the gospel of John, Philip asks Christ: "Show us the Father." Christ responded, "Have I been with you for so long and yet you do not know me.... He who has seen me have seen the Father." (John 14:9). Read what Jesus said, how he acted and what He did. Jesus was not a prophet (a man inside a human body who spoke God's words), but God inhabiting a human body. (Incidentally this is not rocket science; it was a very easy fertilization, similar to cloning, of Mary's egg that produced a human body. Instead of sending a human spirit inside it, He went Himself.) The personality and character of God can be seen in Jesus. You can see the nature of God by looking at Christ and by looking at what He did for you on the cross when He died. He RESCUED YOU.

God came for you. He came *in the only way he could* to legally and factually save you by reuniting you with Himself. He took away your sins, punishment, and the curses and the evil that exist on and in you. The cross was not a place of defeat; on the contrary, it was a place of victory and **compassion**.

Focus on and understand the sacrifice, pain and hardship and the mind-boggling, emotional experience it was for God to do what He did: come for you and me and take what we so richly deserve so He could get us back. God wanted and wants you with all His heart.

Let me repeat: God came for you! *He is not mad at you*. He came to take away what is between you and Him. He came because of love. He loves you. He came to save you and to welcome you into His family.

A last comment about God's love: understanding the immensity of creation—(billions of planets), multiple dimensions, 7 billion people on this planet—it can be hard to think that any person is special or personally loved. However, in the infinite greatness of God He is able and does LOVE us individually and completely…and He has time for each of us as though we were the only one (see section on God's humor).

God is compassionate

The psalmist declared in Psalm 145: 8 & 9, "The Lord is gracious and full of compassion, slow to anger and great in mercy. The Lord is good to all, and His tender mercies are over all his works."

I have seen and lived the compassion, love, acceptance and faithfulness of God. He has stayed with me in awful stuff and huge errors and sin. There is NO ONE like Him.

Even in judgment, He repeatedly warns and coaxes us to leave the sin and wrong ways of our lives. When He pronounces judgment, He is open to changing His mind if we (and even nations) repent (see the book of Jonah). When God does judge and punish—bringing the justice required by our sin—He doesn't enjoy it. Regarding his judgment and punishment upon Judah, God states in Micah 1:8: "Therefore I will wail and howl. I will go stripped and naked; I will make a wailing like the jackals and a mourning like the ostriches…."

After judgment, if a person repents, God is quick to redeem the consequences for good. He sets the repentant person on a new foundation. God will always use your own hard-won lessons to minister to others and make them useful for many.

God is not some mean old codger looking to destroy. He is love and compassion looking to redeem a fallen world, a world He once called "very, very good."

Our God is a God of Action

God's love for you is not distant or passive; it is close and active inside you. Working from within, it transforms you so you can receive His blessings. Through what He did on the cross, what He speaks to you from the Bible, and what He does, **you have His authority and power to have a good life and be well.** God does not take over and rule your life; instead, He enters you, lifts you up, and shows you what you can do to become well, to have the promised abundant life.

The devil subjects humans to the slavery of depression, fear, loss, rejection etc. God does not make you a slave to Him; He does not overwhelm you. He comes alongside and teaches you what to do, strengthens and heals you and makes you *you* through Himself. He gives you reign of your life with Him. In order to be you (a person with free will), you act *with* Him of your own free will. God sets you free. It is God who empowers you to take what He has for you.

God is faithful

I have personally tested God to see if He would stay with me whether I was a professional, a salesman, white collar, blue collar, clean or dirty. Amazing: He stayed with me! And in all my hardship, heartbreak, sadness, loss, and lack of direction, God has remained constant. He didn't desert me in my sin or in my struggles with sin nor did he abandon me when I made mistakes, couldn't forgive, and more.

He'll stay with you

The Apostle Paul concluded that even when we're not faithful, God is faithful because He cannot deny His essence: faithful love.

God is a "Person"

The entire Bible is about God, either directly or indirectly. Within its covers we find:

- God is not just a "force."
- God is not impersonal, just some kind of "power" floating around "out there somewhere" that makes things happen.
- God is a "person" (but not a man) with a heart, emotions, thoughts, personality, desires, will, intelligence, creativity, etc (see Isaiah Ch. 42–66).
- We are created in God's image (Genesis 1:26) – i.e. we are

like Him, which means that He is like us (not in our physical bodies, but in who we were made to be; our interior being is like God's).

- Our similarity makes God comprehensible to us, because He chose to make Himself comprehensible to us.
- He revealed Himself more fully to us when He elected to live in a human body (Jesus).

There is something unique and special about humankind's creation because of its similarity to its Creator, its image-bearing makeup. It is in part signified by *the authority (just as God has authority) God originally gave humans* before the fall, and the authority He returned to us in Christ Jesus.

God is creative

This is one of the areas where we can get lost in our understanding of God. He is creative beyond anything we will ever personally experience, but we can see His creativity and understand some of it through our own or another's creativity. We can also discern its immense power whenever we unleash our own creativity.

I sat in a café in Vancouver, B.C. looking at a large book containing photographs of the universe. I was overwhelmed at the colors, immensity, complexity, beauty, extravagance, engineering (atoms to galaxies), design, bizarreness, boldness, even brazenness of it all. How could anybody do that? Why? Was any good thing **not** tried? And the pictures were only of the physical dimension! How many others exist in the same "space"?

My answerless question was: "What motivated God to do all this?! Can He just not restrain Himself?"

You and I consider an atomic bomb to be powerful; same with the sun, our solar furnace, the engineering and creation of which is far beyond human understanding. Yet, here before me in a solitary book was a manifestation of power, design, engineering, and artistry far beyond our sun and far beyond anything I had ever imagined.

And God created it all. I find it beyond absurd, try as I might, to believe that the intricate design of a cell, of DNA, of a human body or that a planet just "evolved." Clearly such immense engineering feats call for questions: Who is the architect? Who is the builder?

God is creative and powerful beyond anything you or I can fully comprehend. The good news is that He's also good and holy! Our planet and immediate environment would be far more magnificent if they were connected to Him. If He were the ruler of this world, all would work as He designed it to work at the outset: He would have made it work in goodness and holiness, which is in keeping with His character.

A brief note, based on my reading of the power of the Egyptian magicians who stood before Moses, and Satan's power described in Revelations: It appears that some biological machinery can be created by Satan. I suspect that much of the unpleasant insects and other organisms are not the work of the true God. Once allowed in, Satan had and has semi-free reign to mar (and destroy) God's creation, in the act of which he shows us his character. He is the "god" whose nature is destruction, misery, and death (even though he does everything to hide it).

God cares about us

In spite of the phenomenal expanse and greatness of creation, God came to this apparently undistinguished planet, one among billions of other planets, became a man, lived as a man to reveal Himself to us and show us that we are not forgotten or unimportant!

God is a bit wacky

Clearly, God is not straight-laced. Consider: He created the clown fish, the giraffe and the elephant. In Him, all of creation on Earth would have manifested without sadness, sorrow, death, in joy, peace and unity. God's Kingdom is NOT divided or in conflict. Even in its fallen and decaying state (now degraded to the point of evil), the original wackiness of God can be seen. I think it best not to costume God in a Sunday dress suit or in bohemian's garb: He is in a class all by Himself in three persons.

God has a sense of humor

Aside from God's humor manifested through me (an individual and lowly member of his creation commenting on what He did, does and is) I want to share a grand joke that God played on me.

I was in Lima, Peru en route to Ecuador. I arrived late but wanted to go out for a meal. The room clerk advised me to leave everything in the hotel safe except what I needed, so I took $20 dollars and went on my way. Not long after, I was assaulted and the $20 dollars stolen. I went to the police.

I was mad. That night I complained to God. In my heart, I wanted a Christian to *comfort me*, to tell me how nasty these folks were to rob me. But what I **said** to God was: "Father God, send me a Christian."

Before my flight left the next day, I got into a taxi for a tour of the city. The driver, an off-duty cop who was moonlighting, _**would not shut up**_. He spoke of his misadventures and, as the ride went on…sin. I didn't want to hear it; I wanted a tour. But he just would not shut up. For more than two hours I listened to this cop's sins.

When we arrived at the airport, fed up, I asked him if he would like to accept Jesus as his Lord and Savior. Suddenly in tears, He replied "Yes!"

I led him through the sinner's prayer – finishing just as we pulled up to the terminal.

As I reached for the door handle, God spoke to me: "You met a Christian!" I could hear Him laughing. He *knew* that's not what I had meant when I told Him I wanted to meet a Christian; I had wanted to be comforted. The joke was on me.

I didn't know how to react. It seemed unfair. I wondered if there was any way I could return the "Touché" and play a joke on Him without His being able to know all about it beforehand. (Alas. No way! Well maybe, using the Bible to hold His feet to what we want?)

Yes. God has a sense of humor.

God is kind

I've already covered the things God has done to make a way for you to know Him and to receive the good things He has for you: healing, provision, abundant life, etc. He is patient and slow to anger while you and I fumble around. See Exodus 34:6

God is holy

God is holy. There is no evil, no evil tricks, no deceit, no lies, no dirt to soil Him or what He does. He is 100% faultless. He is pristine. His judgment of evil is part of His holiness and goodness. Through Jesus, you and I have escaped punishment because God's genuine anger at evil and destruction was suffered willingly by Jesus so we can be acceptable to God.

God Has Not Abandoned You

Jesus came to unite you with Himself, with the Father and the Holy Spirit. It isn't just that He came, showed you His love by dying for you, later to abandon you – leaving you to fend for yourself.

After Jesus rose from the dead, He returned to live in your heart. (Remember that the spirit dimension is different from this one and that we live in it also.) Jesus inside is no metaphor; He really is inside you, and through His presence you have a new nature: you are a new creation).

No matter how alone, ashamed or convicted you feel, God has not abandoned you. If you've accepted Jesus into your heart, God is there–***truly and actually there as spirit.*** He moves inside your heart, mind and body to direct and heal you. You have become fused to God. In hardship and trauma, we often cannot feel or sense Him, even though He is inside us (cohabiting with our own spirit and the evil spirits who are working against us) directing our thoughts, memories and prayers. John 14:26: "He will teach you all things, and bring to remembrance all things that I said [scriptures and other divine messages] to you."

Through Christ, you've become God's child. You're part of His family. You carry His name. You're protected and loved. You belong to Him. The Bible says in 1 John 3:1: "How great is the love the Father has lavished on us, that we should be called children of God. And that is what we are…!" (NIV)

He also sent the Holy Spirit to live in you. He, together with the fullness of God (Father, Son and Holy Spirit) is with you forever. He is not only with you, but continues to act on your behalf – teaching, counseling, and helping. He is there in every decision, in every part of your life strengthening you, being a true friend.

About the Holy Spirit

The Holy Spirit is the third "person" of the one God. Although present on earth before Jesus' death, he came more fully after His death. John 14:16–18 says, "And I will pray to the Father and He will give you another Helper that He may abide with you forever, even the Spirit of Truth who the world cannot receive, because it neither sees Him nor knows Him, but you know Him, for He dwells with you and <u>will be in you</u>. I will not leave you as orphans, I will come to you."

John 14:23b. "*We* (God the Father, Son and Holy Spirit) will come to him [any person who loves Him] and make our home with him."

The person of the Holy Spirit is good, holy and powerful.

All His directions and actions are, and will be, good and holy. He always directs in purity and goodness. He is never profane, dirty or evil. He is also HOPE, not hopelessness. He came upon Jesus in the form of a dove at His baptism. From my experience, in Jesus, this continues to be His manifestation of character. The Holy Spirit is another person of the One God in three parts. <u>He completes the Spirit power we need to overcome the world, the fallen angels (devils), and our fallen bodies and nature..</u>

Claim the things that God brings to mind. Reject your own thoughts and any thoughts that ungodly spirits place into your mind: impure thoughts, thoughts to do wrong, thought of despair, hopelessness, purposelessness, mental instability, emotional instability and fear. Especially fear. Go with Him, the "ride" will be good.

God Is a Good Guy, Someone Worth Knowing

God is a good guy and indescribably worth knowing. Abraham was his friend; you are, too. God wants all of us to worship Him as God Almighty, but He also wants us to understand that we are His friends.

Never forget: Even though He is Almighty God and you

are his friend, pride should have NO purchase in your heart or mind because no matter how deep your relationship is with Him, he **will** judge sin and wrongdoing; He **will** correct you, just as **any** engaged, loving father would do. Having said this, in His faithfulness, love and fatherhood, you will find peace, love, wise counsel, and eternal friendship.

The whole thing sometimes seems absurd, doesn't it? How can one person, standing on a speck of a planet in an extravagant universe, know God and be His friend (or anything even close)?

King David, too, pondered this question in the eighth Psalm, v. 4, "What is man that you think of him, man that you care for him?"

After all, when was the last time the ruler of your country called and asked to be your friend? Why would the ruler and creator of **everything** want to befriend you or me…to allow us to know Him?

I don't have *that* answer! All I know, from all I've read and from my own experiences, is that this is *exactly* what He wants to do.

I can't begin to understand what God sees in me that He considers it worth the bother. What can I possibly bring to the table?

My conclusion is that His character is love, fatherhood and relationship. He went to the point of moving heaven and earth through His Son's death to reconnect with you and me, because

He places great value on folks like us.

Can it possibly be that God sees us in our defeats, battles and losses and cheers for us – not excusing our sin, but seeing the hordes of dark evil spirits working against us and impossible odds of being saved? The Bible says that it is "easier for a camel to go through the eye of a needle" than to be saved. God, in His love, helps us, the underdogs – choosing us, caring for us?

Crazy love, another comment on the love of God

The love of God is aggressive, self sacrificing, merciful, faithful and caring beyond all measure, reason and emotion. The love of God is like that of a parent who puts all hurt and disappointment behind him and pursues his child.

God has left no stone unturned in his pursuit of you. He sent Jesus to rescue you. And in the continuous **now** He never lets go. He is faithful in His efforts to continually draw you to Himself. When you run down the wrong spirit trails, He stays with you to draw you back to Him.

It is *crazy* love; deeper and better than all joyful or tragic love songs. It is a love from the heart and mind, supported continually by *aggressively kind and loving deeds.* It is the only true love that exists… and *it's yours*! *It's for you.* It's the kind of crazy love every heart desires. And if that's not enough, He's also your friend. He unselfishly wants the best for you. *He likes you,*

He jokes with you (you mostly don't get it), creates weird funny stuff for you (weird "coincidences," ironic situations, and comic events), and He encourages, empowers and makes you who you were meant to be, who you truly are.

He is always with you, continually trying to help you. When you fail (morally or otherwise) and totally give up on yourself and want to die, *He still believes in you* and will put you back on the path of life. He is the cheerful, faithful friend who lifts you up. He has your back at all times: *crazy love, crazy friendship.*

From my point of view, God *is* crazy to love so much. Somehow He can risk caring so much. He can handle it. I suspect that if you and I ever truly understood the love of God we wouldn't survive: our physical hearts would fail as a result of the magnificence of His love. *Why does He care so much?? Why does He care at all??*

God accepts us in His love. He's our Father. In Jesus, he made us His own; He made us part of His family, whether we, or anyone else, recognize it. We bear His name. We are His. He is your parent and He wants to teach, bless, and train you.

Part Three: COMPLETE THROUGH FAITH

Believing that God exists and *knowing Him* are two very different things. Even the devil believes God exists (and trembles as a direct result). *Believing in God* and *believing what He says* are also different.

Total faith is *being absolutely convinced* of something in every part of your being. Faith is strongest and most effective at that level. Some things only happen when one's faith is total. That said, there are various levels and types of faith.

The essential part of your faith is to know God. Right behind knowing God is believing what He says. The most important part of believing what He says is to believe the Bible which is His account of mankind and Himself. Through divine inspiration, God created it and uses it as a living thing. Its function is to instruct you about God, existence, the things of God (what He expects of us), of the world and of evil. Aside from general instruction, He brings passages alive to speak to you. (See the communications section of this book.) He brings laser-like focus and meaning to certain parts of the Bible to confer a specific understanding about what He wants you to know or consider.

The highlighted part may be out of context. For example, when I managed a resort temporarily, I was hyper-critical of the work in certain departments. God highlighted a section of scripture that let me know I could harm "the congregation" (meaning workers in this case), if I continued along the same lines.

Through your relationship with God and your reading of the Bible, faith is the avenue by which you understand the structure of existence and embrace (believe) it. Everything contained in the Bible has a purpose even though it relates to ancient history.

As you read the Bible, you'll find that many of the things of God are contrary to your experience. For example, we've looked at the good and kind character of God within the pages of this book, but perhaps your life experience has given you a different point of view. Faith is believing not only in God, but in Who He is, and what He says. There are many places in the Bible where God says that He is telling the truth. Faith is only faith when you believe without seeing something that has not yet been "proven". As soon as you *see* it, or it *happens*, faith is fulfilled and you may only have to exercise faith to *keep* whatever has happened.

If you allow your life to be controlled by other teachings and/or your senses and reason, based only on what you see or can discern, it will be impossible to understand the things of God and receive the profound blessing He has for you. The person controlled by his senses, experience and reason cannot be convinced. Only when the Word of God (that is the Word of the True God contained in the Holy Bible) controls what you think and understand can you begin to receive what God has for you. Until that happens you'll rely on what you feel, hear, see and understand: the teachings, understandings and conclusions that come from this world.

Belief is like oxygen to water: oxygen is a part of water, but very different. Faith is similar. It has parts which must combine to make it faith rather than mere belief (a component part of faith). In my experience, the Word of God only gains control of my mind (consciousness) when my experience in God, His personal word to me, and my (at least) semi-conscious awareness and/or understanding of something relevant in the spirit world *combine* to cause *faith* to trump the natural (or when the foregoing causes mere belief to become powerful faith; that is, faith in the truth revealed in the Bible).

Faith is the vehicle through which you know and receive from God after sin separated you from Him. Before Adam and Eve fell into sin, they walked with God, faith wasn't necessary: they knew God.

Faith is a spirit "thing". God is a Spirit; faith allows us to connect with Him and with the spiritual. God uses faith to open a path between the two worlds (dimensions). God designed faith. He works through faith according to the laws of faith.

Cautionary Note: Faith in the devil, any desire to know him, and false teaching works similarly. Ungodly faith allows access to evil (through faith you can know the very real devil) and negative faith opens the door to the unwanted (for example: catastrophe).

Characteristics of Faith

Faith is not blind

Faith can come from knowledge, understanding and experience. For example, you have faith that flipping a light switch will turn on lights.

In the things of God, simple faith (willingness to try) is the beginning. Faith is later confirmed through experience, understanding and knowledge.

Often a need, for which there is no solution in the natural, will compel you to look into the faith area. Once motivated, faith is the first "concrete" step that opens up the things of God to you: whether it's a first step to seek Him or advanced steps to grow in your relationship with Him, mature in your new life with Him, and receive the things He has given you as His child. Your initial step of faith in Christ may be nothing more than openness to investigate or explore the things of God through Jesus.

In my case, motivated by a selfish need, I mentally began

to explore the possibility of finding a supernatural or spiritual answer. I listened to Christian radio, through which the reality and person of Jesus was preached. As a result I began to think that Jesus was worth a try. And there were other encouragements, including the conversion of my late wife Maggie a short time before, and her insistence on Jesus. At some point, though, for me this "theoretical Jesus" had to become real. Experience *had to* confirm faith.

As an intellectual, my deep faith was, and is, a process. In the beginning I combined a smattering of faith (about the size of the proverbial mustard seed) with an inquiry. I sought to know if God existed. I encountered Jesus (my spirit to Spirit) in a parking lot in Kona, Hawaii early one morning. He said to me in a clear voice, *"You are saved and I am your friend."* After meeting Him I sought understanding. It came through experience (relationship) with Him. Then I sought to understand the things of God and the "why" of those things (knowledge). In the process, the world and my growing understanding of the spirit dimension began to make sense: the things of God became logical. This progression—from God seeking, to faith coupled with understanding— created a certainty that the things of God were real, and created a desire for them to become manifest and to get what God had for me.

So then, ultimately faith is not illogical or "blind." At some point, God through faith moves unseen reality to a point where you can actually confirm the effects your faith is having in the spirit realm and eventually in the physical realm.

In the case of Jesus, after my encounter, to some degree, *I no longer needed any faith at all* to believe in Jesus: I met Him and I literally discovered that He was then in my heart: I could feel Him and through the spiritual eyes He gave me, I could *see* him inside my chest.

But faith was and is necessary to *maintain* that relationship. I know people who met Jesus but lost their faith in Him and who now remember Him only as a distant, irrelevant part of their lives.

What I am saying is that faith and experiential reality intersect. My encounter through faith was real. It happened to me while I stood in the physical world at a certain physical location, but it was a spiritual experience. Thereafter, through interaction with my own spirit, Life and Love (which we receive in its purest form only from God, because God *is* Life and Love) began manifesting itself in every area of my life.

After achieving a certain level of understanding through this unexpected encounter with Jesus, God began to tell me about the condition of my life and what I needed to know to come out of the heavy bondages I had inherited and also those to which I had opened myself.

For example, although the Bible speaks of devils and demons, it was *after I* **saw** a demon actually take over a person that I had true understanding and knowledge of the existence and operation of demons. I saw the victim's ***body take the form of the devil***, not like the form of a human being but as a complete and clear model of the profane spirit within the physical body. What I witnessed was real and convinced me of the dark part of spirit world.

Faith is the first and key part to your journey with and into God. The things of God are real; they will reveal themselves to you in some very real ways. I have seen and lived the manifested provision of God in my life, from health to economic provision to the writing of this book (which was prophesized many years ago).

Having said all this, there are advanced aspects to faith. Some specific characteristics of faith follow.

<u>Faith is a force.</u> The Bible says that your faith, even faith the size of an almost invisible mustard seed (Matthew 17:20), is sufficient to move mountains. As we can push and move things in the physical dimension, so faith pushes and moves things in the spirit world (dimension). Great faith operates like a bulldozer or crane does in the physical dimension. If it is big enough, obstacles are removed.

<u>Faith is a conduit</u>. Faith is a passageway between the spirit and physical worlds.

The things (and works) of God that exist in the spirit world manifest in the physical by your faith in them. Your faith is the channel that allows spirit things to manifest in your physical world.

Faith also is the interface where God moves on your behalf.

Faith, authority and actions. Earlier I wrote that you have authority over Satan and his power. Luke 10:17 and 19, respectively, say: "Then the seventy returned with joy, saying, 'Lord, even the demons are subject to us in your name'" and "Behold, I give you the authority to trample on serpents and scorpions, and over all the power of the enemy, and nothing shall by any means hurt you." Matthew 18:18 says: "Assuredly, I say to you, whatever you bind on earth will be bound in heaven, and whatever you loose on earth will be loosed (let loose) in heaven." Faith is your enabler; through faith you believe what He says; with it you exercise the authority that God has given you through Christ. Through faith you take actions. By faith you continue doing whatever "it" is until the results manifest, until they become solid and secure for you (i.e. you believe that your existence in God is as He says it is). See Hebrews, chapter 11 regarding faith as an enabler.

Redemption: Faith and the work of the cross

The devil has tried mightily to limit believers' understanding of the extent of the work of the cross and the many blessings and authority you have because of what happened there. We've already looked at what Jesus accomplished on the cross based on the quoted Bible verses. The works include: forgiveness of sins, salvation from sin, eternal life, healing, deliverance from pain, freedom from the curse of the law and transferred authority. The above are the first fruits of the Kingdom of God through Christ and the benefits of His work **living** inside you.

In the spirit world, Jesus **completed** these things (John 19:30); there is nothing else that you or I need to do to "earn" them. There is absolutely no doubt as to God´s will here: He has *already done the work.* The question is: **will you receive it and, if so, how**?

The works performed on the cross were mostly performed *in the spirit world.* It was there that Jesus was saddled with our sin, infirmity, pain, and the curse. It is in the spirit world that Christ's completed work on the cross *is visible* (Isaiah 53 and John 3:15). In the flesh, Jesus was witnessed as a severely beaten man. In the spirit world, he *became* sin (and looked it) and was cast into Hades. Done deal: Jesus was *his*... or so Satan thought! But then Sunday came 'round...

Faith is both the conduit and force which God has given humankind to bring the completed work of the cross (and all spiritual blessing in heavenly places – Ephesians 1:3) into the natural world. It is through faith that Jesus' completed work manifests in the natural. By faith, the work of the cross supernaturally *overpowers* the natural. (The focus here is on healing, provision, and living the promised abundant life.)

Applying the provision of God

The Word of God is spirit, truth and power. Remember: your key to receiving the things of God is the Word of God. Use the Word of God directly. Find the Bible verses, find what is granted in them and *use the verses (and concepts)* by proclaiming them. They belong to you. *They are yours!*

This process requires you to know what God says, and to believe it, stand on it, and not be swayed by circumstances and by what you see and live in the flesh. You must believe that God has what He promises for you, and do what's necessary to receive it. Faith requires deeds (James 2:17). The deeds, tools, weapons and your part are explained in this teaching. You must act on what you learn and continue to seek God on all issues as you go forward in faith.

Roadblocks to faith and receiving from God

It's often the case that a person fails to receive from God even though he or she believes in God's provision, the faith channel is open, and faith is strong enough to work as a force. We've looked at spirit things: remember, they are actual things made of spirit. The spirit, soul and body of some people can be so clogged with harmful spirit things that they can't receive what God has for them.

Perhaps the most important obstacles are disobedience and

unforgiveness. Disobedience is refusing to do what God said, or says, to do. Disobedience can be founded in rebellion, unbelief and extreme need often resulting in a form of idolatry: seeking something or someone to do what God wants to do.

Unforgiveness exists in various forms: refusing to forgive others, not forgiving yourself, not forgiving God, not believing that another person (or yourself) is forgiven. The various forms of unforgiveness are often linked; where there is one, another often occurs.

You and I are **commanded** to forgive. When we receive God's forgiveness we lose the "right" not to forgive (anyone – even ourselves!). If you don't forgive, God will allow you to remain in bondage until you do; the provision of freedom through the cross will be withheld until you forgive. Matthew 18: 32–35 discusses this.

As a parenthetical comment: in order to forgive you may have to come to the understanding that God will replace what was taken, and also that forgiveness does not serve as an enabler. Somehow God will free you even if you forgive!

God, *through immense cost to Himself (the death on the cross of His only begotten Son)*, forgives you; He *expects you to do the same for others*. If you do not or seemingly cannot, you'll remain on the outskirts of God's Kingdom and blessings. Oh, you'll be looked in on constantly, but the decision to forgive remains yours. This is one "thing" God cannot do for you. No matter how difficult it may be to let go and let God handle the justice part of the equation, you <u>can</u> do it through Jesus. Forgiveness is a work inside your heart and spirit—and yes, it can be very hard work!

If you struggle with self-forgiveness, undesirable things will remain in and on you because you find it next to impossible to pardon yourself and to believe that God forgives you also. Your failure to forgive and understand that you're forgiven opens a door (or keeps one open) that the devil will use to keep punishing you. Your infirmities of body and spirit will remain as self-punishment. Note: Your punishment is not from God, because Jesus bore your punishment and paid for it completely (and then some). **Your punishment is in a sense self-inflicted (although evil spirit based). Give it up. God already took it, so why carry it any farther?** It's heavy.

And here's the best part. *Astonishing!* In the eyes of God, your "junk" is not just forgiven, but entirely *forgotten*. Key to a victorious life in Christ is your knowledge of the work of the cross; if you know and remember His work on the cross and take it, you lay claim to the fact that you are right and well with God not because of anything you did or failed to do, but because of what GOD DID. As a believer, you're justified by faith in God's provision (the cross), not by your deeds.

If you don't believe what the Bible says, you can't receive. People who don't believe in Jesus cannot receive salvation. People who believe but don't repent can't receive salvation. It's the same for the other provisions of God: you must meet the prerequisites. Any Christian who doesn't actually believe in the promised abundant life and know how to receive it *can't* receive it. They've bolted the door shut from the inside.

Understand: Your provision for salvation, healing, blessing, deliverance, freedom from the curse and pain *already exists*. You just need to understand how to receive the full benefit of the provision, which requires *knowledge and application*, part and parcel of a manifested faith. The Bible says that if you believe with faith, what you believe will happen here on earth (Mark 11: 23 & 24), subject to removing the impediments that block your receipt of the blessings.

God's Word tells us that Jesus took away your sins, punishment, illnesses, grief, and the curse of the law (the curse of sin) and gave you every spiritual blessing (Eph. 1:3), abundant life, and deliverance. These are FACTS. The provision exists, but for you to receive, *in faith* you must embrace and own the benefits of the cross and the Kingdom of God.

Remember, faith is a spirit thing; part of its function is to be the conduit that connects the spirit world to your physical world. It is by faith that you and I claim and receive what God has done and by faith that the supernatural work done on the cross and its benefits overcomes the natural and we become free.

As I said earlier, God has changed the very structure of your existence based on what he did on the cross. You are no longer just a natural being, but a re-established spirit being (like Adam and Eve were before the fall): you wield the supernatural power of God and can do everything God has given you to do to set yourself and others free; but take note: to the extent you must have the supernatural, you must leave the impeding natural behind. The Bible says that if you live only in the "natural" (earthly) you cannot receive the inheritance that comes through the promises that come through faith (Gal. 4:30).

Further comments about faith as a force

Remember that the spirit world is logical. It's subject to spirit realm laws. The provision of God in the spirit dimension is different from the provision of God in the physical. In the spirit world, you can't grasp things using your physical hands. You function there by using faith and your words and actions. And please note: That is how God created the world, through faith and His Word!

There are many types of faith. Within certain limits, the law of faith functions for everyone, believers and non-believers alike – but again, within the limits established by God. For example, a non-believer can't be freed of sin using faith alone without the provision of the cross. Why? Because sin is a real spirit thing in the life of non-believers and the judgment of God rests on them. Faith can't overcome something that God has established except in ways that God decrees. (This is not surprising. If you want to replace a head gasket on an engine, you have to follow the procedure and use the necessary tools. It is the same in the spirit realm, you got to follow the procedure and use the tools.)

Now, based on the factual and legal work that Christ did for you on the cross, you can use your faith to manifest what God has promised you. For example, by faith you can receive healing. When the conduit of faith is opened, it moves the provision of God to you, making healing possible. So within the limits established by God, faith does heal.

A healed believer has to understand what God has for him or her, and then believe it and receive it with faith. But make no mistake: after the healing the devil will try to mimic or actually return the symptoms of your infirmity, so remember this: *whatever you've received by faith, you must maintain by faith.*

Faith based on the cross of Calvary is greater than the devil and the world because even Satan's functioning must be within the limits God established. Satan is not God's opposite; Satan's equal counterpart is an archangel. God calls the shots. Rest in that knowledge and know that you can win any battle.

Faith: works and acts

When you express your sin before God (confession) you acknowledge your wrongdoing. All believers must acknowledge their sin; the act is non-negotiable. All believers must recognize their wrong ways and ask forgiveness.

Repentance is an about-face; it's all about leaving ungodly (confessed) stuff behind, the stuff that has been tripping you up in the spirit and physical worlds. Renouncing those things is expressing your heart's desire to leave sin and all other un-useful things behind and separating (or beginning the separation process) from them. Sometimes this is easy, sometimes it's very hard.

Just as you can renounce the ownership of a physical thing like a car, you can renounce spirit things; you can give up your ownership of them, but leaving stuff behind can often require lots of work and the Holy Spirit.

To do this, you release them, give them to God, or cut them off. (After signing over the title, you give up possession.) And even when you can't release them in the physical world, you press forward in God. Do this via verbal and mental expressions before God. Sometimes you use physical actions when separating from ungodly things: i.e. you'll take them (symbolically with your hand) from your heart and give them to God. It's often helpful after "reaching" into your heart and taking things out of it to then "replace" the emptied spot within with something that God wants you to embrace (love, forgiveness, purity, etc.). (A brief aside: remove the physical items involved with your sin also; for example, throw away all the pornography if that is your challenge.)

Examples:

"In the name of Jesus, I remove alcohol and replace it with water."

"In Jesus' name, I remove pride and replace it with humility."

"In Jesus' name I remove rebellion and replace it with submission and obedience."

"In Jesus' name, I remove sadness and hurt and replace it with God's love and care."

"With God's blessing and provision, I take unforgiveness out of my heart, mind and soul and replace it with forgiveness."

Declaration of Positive Faith

Use positive expressions to proclaim what the Bible says God has for you as His child. For salvation, healing, freedom from the curse and pain, proclaim and claim the complete work of the cross, even when your physical senses and present experiences seem contrary to the proclamation. For freedom from sin or addictions, declare and believe in your victory over them even though you are not yet free. (And do what is necessary to be free; see the getting help section.) In the spirit world, you appropriate what God has done for you and given you through proclaiming His very real power over your situation; the physical world will have to follow.

It is never foolish to proclaim (verbally, mentally, or physically) over situations, seen or unseen. <u>Your proclamation is your belief in action. But it is not belief based on faith alone, it is belief based on something **real**: on the work that Christ did at Calvary.</u> It is real faith, based on real work that Christ did, and based upon the Word of God (the Bible). The Word of God in your heart and your mouth, combined with your faith, is a force far more powerful than an atomic bomb.

Your words of faith are what put you in a position to receive from God and what puts God in position to move on your behalf. Please understand that your words of faith (declaring what you are not experiencing), can take great effort. John 6:24 says that our work is to believe in Jesus – including what He did for us.

Traps

Beware! The devil sets traps. The devil has real power over your spirit, soul and body; he can make you feel good one day for the purpose of causing you to put your eyes on how you feel rather than on the Word of God. Shortly thereafter the devil will bring back the symptoms or problems and your faith—now weakened because you fixed your eyes on how you are feeling—can't easily withstand the new attack.

Struggle to keep your trust in God´s Word and in God Himself; whether your circumstances agree or not, the Word of

God tells you that on the cross Jesus made a provision for you. Praise Him for the provision, trusting in the promise and power of God. What you expect from God should be on what He says in His Word, not on what your senses tell you. In the process praise Him and tell Him that you trust Him.

Negative Faith

Beware of negative faith. The negative statement of faith that comes from your mouth makes you a prisoner of your own ill-considered words. Positive confession and the Word of God in your mouth put you on the right path. What you say, mixed with your positive faith, puts you on the path to what will become your new reality in Christ.

Regarding negative expressions, the Bible says in Proverbs 6:2, "You are snared by the words of your mouth; you are taken by the words of your mouth."

In the first section of this book we looked at spirit things. As you recall, there are good and bad spirit things – genuine things made of spirit. Satan brings you packages of evil things (e.g. illnesses and temptations). **When you state with your mouth that you own them, it's like signing a receipt for a package the devil wants to deliver to you. Don't do it! Refuse to take delivery.**

Key Scriptures

1. Spirit thing: the Word of God

"My son, give attention to my words; Incline your ear to my sayings do not let them depart from your eyes, keep them in the midst of your heart, for they are life to those who find them, and health to all the flesh." Proverbs 4:20–21

The Word of God is a spirit thing. It is truth, power and medicine. It works by itself as a living spirit thing continually empowered by God. Apply it directly. It also works through giving knowledge and understanding to enable us to grow, change and take the things God gives us.

2. The four Biblical foundations of divine healing.

Jesus took our sins:

"Who Himself bore our sins in His own body on the tree, that we, having died to sins, might live for righteousness - by whose stripes you were healed." I Peter 2:24

Jesus took our infirmities and pains:

"Surely He has borne our griefs and carried our sorrows, yet we esteemed Him stricken, smitten by God, and afflicted." Isaiah 53:4

Jesus took our punishment:

"He was bruised for our iniquities, the chastisement for our peace was upon Him, and by His stripes we were healed." Isaiah 53:5

Jesus took the curse for not doing what God's rules (law) require:

"Christ has redeemed us from the curse of the law, having become a curse for us for it is written, 'cursed is everyone who hangs on a tree.'" Galatians 3:13

Jesus took away everything that stood between you and God. Death was removed and taken to hell. Jesus left it there. Redemption, restoration and healing were given.

3. We no longer HAVE to sin; God made a supernatural foundational provision.

"...our old man was crucified with Him, that the body of sin might be done away with, that we should no longer be slaves to sin." Romans 6:6

4. We have a new source of Power and Strength.

"...which is Christ in you...." Col. 1:27

5. We have died to loving the pleasures of sin and to our ungodly self.

See Romans 6:2, 6:6, 6:9, 6:11 and 2 Cor. 5:17

6. We are a new creation.

"Therefore if anyone is in Christ he is a new creation…."
2 Cor. 5:17

7. Faith –a spiritual force

"For assuredly, I say to you, whoever says to this mountain, 'Be removed and be cast into the sea', and does not doubt in his heart, but believes that those things he says will come to pass, he will have whatever he says." Mark 11:23

8. Faith: a channel between the natural and spirit world (dimension).

"Therefore I say to you, whatever things you ask when you pray, believe that you receive them, and you will have them." Mark 11:24

9. We have supernatural authority and power over the natural world.

Remember Peter walking on water? Matthew 14:29

10. Victory is ours through Jesus inside us, the work of the cross and by our faith.

"You are of God, little children, and have overcome them, because He who is in you is greater than he who is in the world." I John 4:4

11. Nothing is difficult for God.

"Then great multitudes came to Him, having with them those who were lame, blind, mute, maimed, and many others; and they laid them down at Jesus' feet, and He healed them. So the multitude marveled when they saw the mute speaking, the maimed made whole, the lame walking, and the blind seeing; and they glorified the God of Israel." Matthew 15:30–31

12. The reason for everything.

"He sent His word and healed them, and delivered them from their destructions." Psalm 107:20

Christ is the Word and through the Word we are freed. John 1:1&2

Part Four: DELETE: YOUR OLD WAY OF THINKING AND UNDERSTANDING

The Western world has failed to see and understand the spirit dimension; as a sad result, many walls of protection have collapsed, allowing Satan and his hosts of evil to overwhelm our society like a tsunami. The evil ones hate being exposed, hate when their tactics are revealed, and hate even more that you now know God, that you know how to defend yourself (more tools coming in Part Five), and that you are on the offensive to get what God has given you. If you react negatively to the teachings in this book, **please** just consider the possibility that the source of your discomfort may be from spirits that fear being disclosed.

The truth is that you're bombarded by evil beings hell-bent on conforming you to their distorted agendas. Your environment is intense. Our own spirits, souls and bodies are continually subjected to input from the spirit dimension. The input is in the form of thoughts, spirit "pressure" (applied directly to our spirits, souls and bodies) from local spirits, and by pressure exerted by the spirits in the air (the powers and principalities mentioned in Ephesians 6:12). Our minds and spirits are also influenced by the continual ungodly demands of our fallen body.

What we accept, believe, and conclude from our thoughts and experiences form our perception of reality. It is, by definition, a subjective reality, i.e. *our* individual reality. The entire host of evil is there to mold our subjective reality so we fail to understand Who God is, who we are, what He has for us now and in the future, *and* how to live it. Satan and his hosts want us to live their reality so they can manifest through us. God wants our perception of our situation in Jesus to be true and correct so we can experience and receive Him and what He has for us.

The importance of understanding our environment and the players

Someone I know is fond of saying, "The way you see it – so it must be." That's a profound statement. Reality remains subject to each person who interprets it. How you perceive reality will govern you. What is your own point of view?

God wants you to understand what He's **saying** so your subjective (understood) view **coincides** in truth with the natural, spiritual and supernatural reality (life) that God has opened for you to live in. Jesus said, "I am the truth, the way and the life." When you live what God has for you in the way He makes for you, what you take by faith and your reality (life) become *the same.* You live in the fullness of the life God has given you through and in Jesus.

In Romans 12:2b, Paul lays out the principal when he says, "…be transformed by the renewing of your mind…." We have to understand, think, and ultimately live *according to the truth* of what God has given us.

Peter, the impulsive (perhaps unstable) fisherman got it. He left his prior understanding (which was reality for him) and the constructs that governed his life and went on to confirm Jesus' work on the cross and God's love through signs, wonders and miracles. In his first letter, Peter says in the first chapter, verse thirteen: "Therefore, gird up the loins of your mind…." -- that is, keep your mind strong, prepared and protected.

Grab what God is saying here: you need to protect both your mind and its strength to gain life in God and experience your true God-given reality. This is how we begin to live in the promised *supernatural* provision and life that God teaches in the Bible.

So the challenge is to *understand* God, His purpose, what he has done and to believe. When you do, your understanding through faith will open a new reality for you – and a corresponding new life!

Before I met Jesus, I didn't take into account the existence of any God, much less a God Who could know me and who I could know (a real person). Yet that God **and** the host of evil were already working in my life. And although I was surrounded by a spiritual dimension, I didn't realize it, nor did I know I was controlled by spirits.

In a very real sense, my life was a play. I lived as directed by evil. I was an actor playing the part that Satan assigned to me. The part I played was not the real life available in and given by God, but a sub-life created in a bubble. I accepted evil's tale as true life much like Jim Carey in "The Truman Show" accepted his life. As he was in the movie, I was an actor in a created life which was not the life truly available – it was created by lies and sleight of hand. But like Carey in the movie, the possibility existed to understand and to open the door and see and live the real life available outside the bubble. That is what God offers us in Jesus Christ. (See the movie.) The only correct understanding I had was that I lived in a human body. I lived a life based upon a complete lack of understanding of my true condition. I was living tragedy and my manifest life was largely fantasy: I became a sexy pirate smuggler to make living in the bubble tolerable.

At the moment I met Jesus, I grasped that *everything* I had built my life on was false – my conclusions and how I saw everything were based on certain misunderstandings and on an elementary, even primitive, level of knowledge. (Note Isaiah 65:2b.) The moment I encountered Jesus and heard His voice, I *knew* that my life was *all wrong*. Shortly after that I learned about evil spirits and how they had controlled me from birth.

The process of my salvation has largely been a process of understanding my environment, the players, and what God has done to take me from where I was to the promised abundant life (still continuing on) and finally into heaven. For me, it was necessary for Him to teach me what I needed to know to navigate in this world and in the spirit world successfully *and* in truth.

It has been work to leave the theater of my mind and body behind and successfully live the life God wants for me. It has also been the process of learning that God is God – a real God with limitless power who cares for me, and that I am loved, **truly** loved.

The point is that God has a good and abundant life for us in and through Jesus.

Key Tool...faith

As I mentioned before, belief is to faith what oxygen is to water. In your walk with God into His world and into truth, seek faith. Develop faith and get understanding. They are some of the most important tools, along with love and hope. People can believe something but not have the faith to get it. I see it all too often, and have lived it myself, having been defeated by Satan and robbed of what God had for me even as a child. Note, that the application of faith – walking it out, living it, takes *effort*. God has made a way for you, but you have to take it. If you are waiting for God to do your part, you will lose to the devil. I see it all the time.

The good news is that, in His mercy, God has a wonderful

consolation prize which is, in fact, the BIG prize: even when we lose individual battles, as long as we keep our relationship with God, we win – because we go to heaven. This is a core manifestation of the love of God. But as long as we are in our bodies, we should fight. As we do, we can win not just the war between heaven and hell, but win right here, right now, in our earthly lives.

Kenneth Copeland says he plays until he wins. During war, a country can suffer huge losses and defeats, as the U.S. did in World War II to Japan, but still win the war.

Decide to go with and into Jesus and what He says. Take no other exit. Fight the good fight so your particular war ends only after the enemy is *defeated*. **Keep at it until you win.**

Bottom Line: you can get there from wherever you are, no matter how damaged you are, no matter how impossible it seems in the natural. Review the stories of Abraham and Moses. They started too late and only achieved what God had for them by living the supernatural. I'm laying out the principles of your existence and showing you how to manage things so you can live the life that God has for you.

Be Proactive: Understand, do and take the life that God has for you

The Bible and Christian books that God brings you instruct

you in your life and adventure with God. Do what they say. Seek God, seek understanding and seek faith, but remember that the Bible teaches that the good life that God has for us is balanced (see Proverbs), doing spiritual *and* physical things. Don't get weird and far out. A good, healthy Christian community (church) will help you sort through the issues. They'll help you live life in the here and now in peace and joy.

In your struggle, the entire contingent of evil in the spirit world that's working against you *will* discourage and tire you, and if possible, *they will* drag you back into unhappiness, sadness, unbelief, and sin. There will be many times when the whole process seems hopeless – too many issues: heart issues, losses, sadness, and physical issues. Often the things in our hearts seem bolted there; we *can't* release them. The stuff that's battling for control is so deeply rooted that it prevents and/or destroys the very life you're trying to live as a child of God. My advice: do the best you can, keep going forward no matter how exhausted you feel: God is with and for you and—remember that *Jesus has already won the war for you.* By keeping this in mind, perhaps it will be easier for you to continue until you do win the battle.

Satan's strategy is to convince you that your situation is impossible to improve and your problems are greater than God's ability to resolve them. Not true!

Using illness as an example, the devil will tell you the reasons you're sick, or will bring on symptoms to reinforce his position. Please Note: **It isn't that the symptoms or illness (or other problems, addictions, etc.) don't exist;** <u>to the contrary, they do exist because of sin.</u> **But in Christ you have the supernatural power of God to overcome them.** Move your focus from the natural to the supernatural! The cure/remedy to every ill rests in Christ.

I want to add something personal at this point. At one time I was so depressed I continually had to give my disability to God. In my emotional state, I could have gone on Social Security Disability and triggered the company disability policy. Instead I continued forward and claimed God's healing. At another time my skin was so tender and injury-prone that I could only work in the lightest of clothing. Just before my skin became so bad, God placed me and my family in tropical Mexico where the proper attire was light weight clothing! I worked for a U.S. company part time, where my salary was sufficient to allow me to run a Christian Fellowship Center without salary. So God not only provided a *good income* for us, he used me as a missionary in spite of my skin problem. Through the environment and faith my skin was eventually restored. At another time, I'd come to an economic dead end and could only proceed by making *very* difficult, dangerous and humbling changes in direction. In these circumstances, I made the conscious decision to go on with God. As a result, I lived a much better life than one would expect from the natural consequence of my mental state, physical health, and economic position.

What you allow yourself to think and believe is very important. Watch over what you think and everything you say. Focus like a laser beam on God's promises, exclude all else, and you can't be led astray by the wiles of the devil. "The way a man thinks, so shall he be."

Denial and Having Faith are Different Things

Illness, problems and poverty will exist in this fallen physical world until the end. They are real things. To deny their existence would be insane. The issue isn't that they exist, but that the believer, in Christ, has supernatural access to God's provisions.

Like all things of God, if someone doesn't believe in God and His provision, he or she cannot receive it. It isn't that God doesn't **want** to share; it's that His clueless ward has refused delivery, has shut and locked the door from the inside!

Bottom line: Our God is not a gate crasher. We have free will. We get to say no. Too many do.

While ministering to a destitute church in Mexico, the Holy Spirit told me that most of its people didn't believe what God had for them financially. He told me the people wouldn't receive what He wanted to give them because, in some cases, they didn't believe they should prosper financially, and in others, they would not make the necessary changes. They did not take a job I arranged for them because they didn't feel comfortable with a 45 minute prepaid bus ride. They remained in poverty. In some form they didn't believe God, so they didn't exercise the small amount of faith that was necessary to do the acts that would have changed their lives. It's true! What God had for them was a simple process that didn't even require great faith...just *some* faith.

The congregation's response to God: ***Package refused. Return to Sender. No one here wants money. Thanks very much anyway.***

For the people of God to receive, the Christian has to **believe** in God's provision, **act** on what God says, and **claim** what God offers. That is, we (the believers in Jesus) have to **have faith.** In the case of work, it may be that God directs someone to study, change jobs, tithe, or otherwise put his/her self in a place where God can act to bless them financially. In all cases, there is a measure of having to do what God says in a specific situation.

It may, and probably will, take time to receive what God has for you, but the believer has to continue on in faith, not stopping, not going back. God's provision will manifest as soon as God can get all of the pieces in their proper places. In cases with a large physical component, like work, there may be a series of steps so it will take time.

In all provisions of God, there are interacting factors. To

become well, we looked at the role of forgiveness in being able to receive healing. To get the things God has for you, it's essential to control ungodly thoughts, words and actions. Beware, what you and I were once slaves to and have been freed of, should we return to them, we'll be doubly or triply enslaved. Your walk of faith must be a road of no return. We achieve victory by leaving all that crummy stuff behind.

In the case of money, the Bible says that if a person gives a little, he will receive a little. Acting in faith requires believing and acting on what the Bible says. If you as a believer don't act with faith while giving, thereby fulfilling what the Word of God says, you won't receive the full economic provision of God.

A final note: Sometimes God simply tells us what to do or not to do. I realize that it is often hard to know if it is God speaking; but the things God says may be the key to His provision at that moment. Example: I was skiing with my granddaughter and her friend. Before the last run I felt that God told me not to take the last run, that there would be an injury. Instead of stopping, I prayed for protection. The friend fell and broke her wrist.

Faith and Grace

In everything related to faith, there is no open door to do wrong. **Grace**—unmerited favor, forgiveness of sin through

Jesus and relationship with God the Father through Jesus' death—**is not a license to sin.** As a redeemed child of God, you are to make every effort to do right, to reflect His nature, power and presence.

When you do fail (sin), grace gives you ample room to live before God without punishment (although there are natural consequences). Part of God's grace at the time of your sin is to give you knowledge of right and wrong and the desire, and ultimately the power, to do what is right.

Because God is PERFECT, His acceptance of you outside of Jesus would only be possible if you *always* did right 100% of the time. One wrongful "hiccup" (sin) would make you unacceptable. Yikes! Aren't you glad God made a way? (The way is grace.)

The truth is, you and I break God's rules every day. We frequently do wrong. From God's perspective, no one is a "good person." He certainly doesn't weigh our good and bad on a scale and let us connect with Him and go to heaven only if the good outweighs the bad. That's a big relief; no one could ever get there otherwise!

The Bible contains many passages about humankind's duties. The Ten Commandments set the standards: do not murder, do not steal, etc. Other commandments include the duty to love; see Romans 12:1 & 2 and 9–12, see also 13:8. The duty to submit to governing authorities (but not as an excuse to reject Christ) is mentioned in Romans 13:1–7. Homosexuality is condemned in the Old and New Testaments (see Romans 1:26–27), as are bestiality and other sins. Sexual immorality is dealt with in many places in the Bible and mentioned in 1 Corinthians 10:8.

Balance and Being Grounded

I've covered much about the environment you live in and God's provision. You live in both the physical and spirit worlds. In all you do, you need to be grounded in both worlds. However, since you live in a physical body, most of your focus has to be on the physical world while *never* forgetting (and managing) what's going on in the spirit world.

In the physical world, you need to do the activities of daily living the best you can. I suggest your first focus, every day, should be the Lord: read the Bible, pray and praise Him (this is part of managing the spirit world). I do this for about an hour before I get out of bed, but you should do it however long you can; if you're just starting out, perhaps just five or ten minutes every day. After that you'll need to bathe, exercise, care for your family, go to school, prepare for work, or whatever your "job" is: fulfill your duties, participate in society, etc.

I've known many Christians who focus on the things of God, but have no balance; they lack grounding in the physical world. They're lazy, do their work poorly or they don't work at all.

Others are *improperly* on welfare or disability (without being truly disabled), or they otherwise (even though they're working) aren't grounded in a healthy life. These folks focus a lot on God, talk of God, but they often have gaping holes in other parts of their lives from the imbalance and lack of grounding in their physical lives. As a result, in spite of their efforts, they're not very effective in their Christian lives…or worse: they're actually destructive.

Human life should be balanced. God molds us through the events and work of our lives as well as through our experiences with Him. When life is balanced, it gives God a chance to work in multiple areas: work, social, religious, physical, etc. so that He can give us an even greater and more *abundant* life.

If balance is impossible because of your health, jail time, job loss, or other circumstances beyond your control, do the best in the situation you find yourself and trust God. He is able to ground you in difficult circumstances which are beyond your control. Seek balance where and when able. If you are unproductive, through Jesus seek productivity.

An additional comment about grounding: You may never be able to get grounded if you approach life the way you've been taught up till now. We all approach life the way we were taught by our families and/or early childhood environment. We learned family ways of doing things. If your learned mindsets and methods are ungodly and/or filled with error, your success will lie beyond immense roadblocks.

The solution: give up the ungodly and/or un-useful mindsets, habits, attitudes, philosophies <u>and ways of approaching life that you learned in your family and societal environments or that you took on to cope.</u> Learn new ones. This will mean giving up (renouncing and releasing) your identity and trading it in for your new identity as God's kid. (Please see related section on masks, lies, identities, and acting in Part Five.)

If the things you've learned are particularly "off," no one may take you into their group to show you another way. If this is the case, and *if you are willing,* God your heavenly Father will also take up being your earthly father and show you a new way of life. He will do this through what you experience every day, and what He will show you as you read the Bible. You will have to give him everything he asks you to hand over along the way and accept a new mindset (which He will teach you) about work, social interaction, ways of communication, emotional response, habits, diet, and more. From inside you, He will give you the direction, the strength and the power to make the changes you need.

Another reason for good grounding in daily life is that the understanding and conscious awareness of your true environment will be **mind-blowing.** Good grounding in the natural helps you keep mental and life balance.

A Key Hope and Provision: Supernatural Blessings of God

In addition to the new life we receive in Jesus, the authority granted to us, and the new reality God gives us to live in, there are God's other types of blessings. "Blessed is everyone who fears the Lord [who knows that He is God and tries to please Him], who walk in His ways [who do as God indicates and becomes like Him in character]…You shall be happy and it shall be well with you." Ps. 128: 1 & 2b.

Blessings are actions of God that bring good things into our lives. Here I'll deal with two types of God's blessings. The first are specific personal actions that God does for a specific person. The second types of blessing are more general. Both occur because of who God is, what God does, or because of what He instructs us to do or be so that things will turn out well and we'll receive His blessings. Don't lose sight of the fact that God rewards those who seek Him (Hebrews 11:6). He loves you and wants to reward you for seeking conscious good relationship with Him.

Regarding specific blessings: during uncertainty, change, trauma, etc, it's very important to remember that God has great power to provide for you. I've experienced His power, both great and small. It is wonderful when it comes – some kind act, a gift, some small joy. Never forget that God can reach into your life at any moment in a specific way to change things. He is all powerful. In a sense, blessings are our hope in times of great hardship.

The second type of blessing is the type that naturally flows from God because of His character: life provisions of various types. To some extent God gives these to everyone, however, if our actions are right, our words correct, and our character like His, we receive *more* of them. Our very godliness with its wisdom, skills and love bring them to us. God says that they come from Him to those who fear Him and walk in His ways.

The two types of blessings referred to aren't the only types we need when we're counting on God for a miracle or immediate provision. There are blessings which greatly depend on applying the teachings I've shared here. They make Christians capable of receiving and keeping the good things that God has for them.

The point: All of our "things and stuff" must first be about God. God opened a door for us to live a new life and has the wherewithal to provide whatever we need to live well in it. God has the *desire* and *power* for us to live well. This is so important to remember whenever we feel any degree of desperation. Keep going forward; understand what God is saying and how to get what He has for you. Use the tools explained in this book. In your struggle He will provide something for us to hold on to and He'll ultimately give us a good life.

In the natural world and in the spirit world Christ

(Jesus) did the following that allows us to receive His supernatural provisions.

- At the moment of His death, Christ did certain real things at a moment in time and history at a place called Calvary which legally changed the status of all those who belong to Him and are in Him.

- At the moment of His death and completed upon His resurrection, through Jesus, God made a way to remove our sins and the stains of sin that separate mankind (and all of earthly creation) from Him.

- Christ made a provision to deal with our fallen nature and fallen bodies (our independence and sin-saturated selves).

- Christ did not put an end to the laws; on the contrary, through the law, He legally (without violating the Moral Law, Spiritual Law or Physical Law – Matthew 5:17) opened a path so that we could leave sin and the rule of the world and enter into the freedom of salvation of our whole being. This includes authority over evil, the presence of Life in our being, divine healing, growing freedom from sin, and eventually a new body in a new and/or remodeled earth.

- All that Christ did and gained when He died on the cross legally and morally (God does not violate His own standards and laws) belong to all those who are in Him.

- The greatest part of the work of Christ occurred in the spirit world. I Peter 2:24 says: "...who Himself bore our sins in His own body on the tree, that we, having died to sins, might live for righteousness - by whose stripes you were healed." Isaiah 53:4–5 says: "Surely He has borne our griefs and carried our sorrows; yet we esteemed Him stricken, smitten by God, and afflicted. But He was wounded for our transgressions, He was bruised for our iniquities; the chastisements for our peace was upon Him, and by His stripes we are healed."

- In the spirit world, the spiritual works performed by Christ on the cross were visible. The Bible says in Isaiah 52:14: "Just as many were astonished at you, so His visage was marred more than any man, and His form more than the sons of men." In John 3:14, the Bible says, "And as Moses lifted up the serpent in the wilderness, even so must the Son of Man be lifted up."

- Christ was made sin (serpent) and died, taking with Him not just our sins but our sicknesses and grief.

- Christ's death on the cross removed the barriers between God and us (if you accept His death for you).

- The things that Christ did are both spiritual and physical. The spiritual works of Christ exist in the spirit world.

- Christ opened the door to God at His death and resurrection.

- Christ became a multi-dimensional man after His death. He ate food then walked through a wall.
- In Christ and through the Holy Spirit, we can consciously and legally live in the physical and spiritual dimensions.
- Christ took the keys of death.
- Christ has been given ultimate authority over heaven and earth.
- Christ has given us authority and power to say and do in the natural and spirit worlds whatever is necessary to receive the abundant life promised by Him.

Key Things to Understand

Your life consists of living in both the natural and spirit worlds. Everything that happens to you and me is the consequence of (1) something that happened, or is happening, in the natural world, in the spirit world, or in both, (2) the effects of the law on one or the other, or of both worlds, (3) the results of the Cross, (4) the consequences of the acts of a specific spirit or spirits (including, of course, God), and (5) our own actions or inactions (both in the physical and spiritual dimensions).

As an aside, a good example of the effect of actions in the spirit world on the natural is found in the book of Job verses 1:15 – 19.

For the born-again Christian, the work on the cross of

Calvary made a fundamental change in <u>the very structure of our existence</u> which resulted in a change in the function of the spiritual and natural laws. Through the Cross, we have left application of the Laws for the purpose of salvation, and we live in grace and are empowered with authority over our fallen natures, bodies and over other forms of evil and, to an extent, are given power and authority over the natural. The salvation of the cross has connected us to God and makes us heirs to all that God has for his children. It also made Him our Friend.

"For I am persuaded that neither death nor life, nor angels nor principalities (ruling spirits) nor powers (devils), nor things present nor things to come... shall be able to separate us from the love of God which is in Christ Jesus our Lord." Romans 8:38

The Ball is in Your Court

Tools

- Seek to be close to God.

- Pray - ask God to protect you and yours.

- Keep praying the things that God puts on your heart and into your spirit to pray for *until* they are no longer there and you have peace that the work of prayer has been completed in the spirit. (Note, prayer is not just asking God; *things are rearranged in the spirit world by prayer.*)

- Read the Bible to push Satan from your mind.

- Refuse in faith to receive or suffer something that the Bible says we don't have to receive or suffer. Refuse sadness, mourning, insanity, sin and death.

- Exert correct authority to refuse entrance of evil in your life and into your family's lives.
- Sever ungodly spiritual and physical ties with people, things and spirits.
- Close open windows and doors through which evil can access you and those you're praying for, especially your family and those you minister to or who are under your covering.
- Cast off the spiritual hooks that have been thrown onto and into you *and* those you pray for.
- Cast to the ground ungodly and un-useful words that have left your mouth.
- Cover people with Jesus, His blood, in His Name.
- Cast off Satan from you and others through binding and loosing.
- Renounce death and every death wish and close the windows and doors of death to yourself and your family, loved ones and those you minister to.
- Renounce and release all ungodly things, connections, and desires as detailed in this section of this book.
- Choose life for all that is life and Life.
- Choose death to sin and all that is sin.
- Allow your ungodly self to die through Jesus' death.
- Respond to what God says.
- Ask, receive and use your spiritual gifts.

- Claim the things that God has given you.
- Worship God.
- Thank God for your present life.
- Thank God for all else.
- Praise God in all things.
- Trust God and tell Him you trust Him even when you don't – STATE YOUR TRUST NO MATTER WHAT IS HAPPENING.
- Speak of the things of God.
- Invite and speak Jesus into everything.
- Put on the spiritual weapons listed in Ephesians chapter six.
- Big weapon: Laugh!! In fighting death and homicide spirits, laughter pushes them aside. Laughter will take control of you instead of death spirits.
- Fast (don't eat): the atomic bomb of spiritual weapons. The best fast consists of water only but do what you can… and do it often.

Complete warfare

If your life is anything like mine was before Jesus—unspeakable generational spirits, wrong teaching, not having a clue about proper behavior or wisdom, the child of an alcoholic father and a mother with a spirit of insanity (but that did not always control her) and broken family; a child with a sense of abandonment (the road was my home) that resulted in my spiritual access windows and doors hanging wide open—your walk into God's life will be one of heavy warfare. The spirits and spirit stuff will battle mightily to keep you angry and/or impotent and trapped. As you enable yourself in God, they'll torment you, openly or subtly bombarding you with wrong information, wrong views, and wrong actions at every junction, and continually flooding your soul with unsettling emotions, thoughts, desires and memories, then condemning you for them.

It can be, and at times will be, very discouraging. All of the wrong teaching and experiences present in your soul, and the continual wrong information the spirits feed you will result in mistakes, lost opportunities, lost progress and the loss of things you're entirely capable of achieving in Jesus. If you've been in deep sin, or were born to parents in deep sin (ungodly sex, drugs, insanity, witchcraft, homicide, thievery, etc.), or both, then in addition to attacks from those types of spirits, you'll be unusually vulnerable because of open spirit windows and doors through which Satan is driving you toward ruin and/or tragedy.

But don't give up!

When you're weak and beaten down, the battle will manifest in its fullness: Satan will steal things, bring loss and heartbreak.

You may find yourself in even worse sin. When it happens, don't pray for death, because during this time *you are being allowed by God to witness the manifestation of evil*; don't be discouraged by what you see. Through your trials, God will help you understand your tormenters (defiled spirits) so you can beat them, so you can *humiliate and disgrace* them for all to see. God and you as a team will beat them! It just takes time. Keep applying the lessons you've found in this book. Do the best to choose right *today and every day.* Take it one day at a time, making right decisions you can make at any moment (even following bad decisions). When you have victories, share them with others who need to hear them. God will use you even when you lose individual skirmishes.

Steps to Defeat Evil and More Things You Need to Know

Remembering that the spirit world is heavily controlled by words, in this section what I've written should be spoken aloud. What you say during the following section will begin to (and sometimes may completely) sever evil desires, cut ties and bondages, break relations with spirits, and sever hurtful and / or un-useful ties with human beings. Words also break curses.

INSTRUCTION: When you see (for example) "In the name of Jesus Christ, I forgive all those who have offended me," you are to repeat the same aloud. Do this while you're alone.

Obtaining freedom is a battle. *The believer conquers the world and the devil little by little, step by step, moving forward in faith.* Understand: The devil will make every effort to prevent you from saying the words at all, much less say them from your heart; or he'll try to persuade you to delay the process in the hope that you never get back to it. He will also try to convince you to re-adopt those things you have already renounced.

Be wise. Remain constant and continue the process. Getting free is something that you should do, in at least small measure, every day. For some people this is the beginning of something new; for others, it is just another step on the road to more of God.

Often you may have to force yourself forward. Don't be discouraged; the process takes considerable time. **The Holy Spirit will be with you to guide you**. (He is guiding you through the present teaching!) The devil will try to convince you that what is written here is not of God. Struggle to understand and keep the faith so you don't fail for lack of knowledge.

I'll begin with the issue of forgiveness and move on from there to other issues. Say aloud what is written.

"In the name of Jesus Christ, I forgive all those who have offended me, be it family, friends, churches, Christians, Christian leaders, co-workers, countries, government, politicians or any other person. I also forgive myself for all I have done to myself, to others, and for all my errors."

"In the name of Jesus Christ, I break all ties to the spirits of my ancestors, to 'saints,' and to all types of spirits except God. I renounce and break all ungodly ties and all ties not approved by God, especially lust and sexual ties to any and all persons except my spouse."

"In the name of Jesus Christ, I break all curses that are over me and my family. I also break all curses that have come through my mouth that are not godly."

"In the name of Jesus Christ, I close all doors and windows of evil and all addictions that exist in my life and in the lives of my family."

"In the name of Jesus Christ, I renounce the following:

* All that is not holy
* The hooks of sin
* The hooks of women
* The hooks of men
* Sadness
* Illnesses
* Depression
* Death
* Sexual immorality, whoredom and prostitution

* Lust

* Homosexuality

* Pleasure spirits

* Fear

* Television and movies that do not honor God

* Unbelief

* Drugs

* Alcohol

* Music that does not honor God

* Blood pacts (except with Jesus Christ)

* Oaths

* Blood of others

* The blood of birth

   (I only accept the blood of Jesus Christ)

* Hate

* Pride

* Ungodly anger

* Independence

* Vengeance

* Oath of previous marriages

* Unforgiveness

* Being unworthy

* Unholy ties

* "Spiritual" knowledge that does not come from God

* Perversity

* Pornography
* Bad deeds
* Resentment
* Ties with evil
* Ties with death
* Ties with hell
* Ties with the occult
* Ties with spirits
* Spiritual ties to other religions
* Ties with "saints" and "virgins"
* Ties with demons and devils
* Sexual sins
* Rebellion
* Doing it "my way" outside of God
* Envy
* Self Destruction except thru the cross of Jesus
* Destruction
* Speaking evil of people
* Being critical of people
* Murder - through physical and/or verbal force
* Self destruction except through the cross of Jesus
  (through which we die to sin and ungodly self)
* Ungodly spiritual ties with any church and/or religion
* Erroneous teachings
* Erroneous doctrines
* Ungodly music and dancing to ungodly music

* Hurt
* Distrust
* Rejection
* Inferiority
* Inadequacy
* Unfriendliness
* Divorce
* Self abuse
* Violence
* Manipulation
* Piracy
* Cruelty
* Perversion
* Being evil
* Being materialistic
* Greed
* Being a "self made person"
* Being a child of any other god or spirit
* All else that is unholy and/or un-useful
* Add whatever you need to add

After renouncing (out loud) the foregoing, say: "Jesus Christ, I invite you to fill all the places where these things exist or have existed."

Release

A decision to forgive or take another action (e.g. renounce unforgiveness) serves to correctly orient yourself before God and get rid of many things in your life. It's also part of repentance. But there are things inside you that, although renounced, may not have been released because a part (or parts) of you remain bound to them. This is a dicey area.

Forgiving (with your mouth) someone or even an entire society that has deeply wounded you doesn't necessarily mean that the offense and hurt are released. The same is true of ungodly anger and other sin; the desire and actions of renunciation do not *always* extinguish the matter.

As in the case of renunciation, release is a decision, *but it takes a deeper level of decision and effort.* It starts by telling God that you renounce and release a matter even as you make a *heart effort and decision* to release the matter. Let go. Ask Him to help with whatever you can't release. Often what can't be released is tied to numerous areas of the soul, body and spirit. It is part of who we are (for example: an angry person, a fearful person, a lustful person, a proud person, successful, a failure, a bum, rejected, etc.); it requires an entire change within every area of our being in order for us to become the new creation the Bible tells us we are.

Here, again, the heart is key. In your struggle, you have

to make a whole heart decision to trust God and to go into and onto the new with Him. It is a very personal thing between you and God and **IT IS NOT EASY**. Keep at it. Remember to take bad things out of your heart and put godly things in with a hand motion. The Benefit: Heart cleaning and release allows you and God to empower the God stuff and also put new things into it. You will not be left empty to feel orphaned or in any other way lessened; instead, you will be filled with the new, truly good things which only come from God. James 1:17

Moving on – Further renunciation and release

A part of renunciation and release is to understand how the spirits work and refusing to "follow" them down the path they want you to travel. Recognize the road at the beginning, confirm the renunciation and release, and don't go with them. For example, in the case of anger, don't even begin to get angry. Don't start down that road, catch yourself at the beginning. If allowed the spirits will take you to murder.

As mentioned in the first part of this book, the spirits want you to "run" with them. There are all kinds (families) of spirits to "run" with: proud spirits, violent spirits, perverse spirits, sad spirits, death spirits (a lot of these), sexual spirits, pleasure spirits of all types, lazy spirits, and on and on. They want to lead you and also get you to frequent or live in geographical areas they control.

An example is a spirit (not Holy Spirit) led desire to drink alcohol. (Drinking wisely itself is not sin, if you have no addiction and it does not open you to sin). A susceptible person goes along with the spirit-led thought of drinking. After the first drink, the person accepts the idea of another couple drinks. Not long after, the spirits (from my observation, they usually run in groups) then suggest dancing at a respectable place (so why not go out)…

Some of the dancers are sexy. The drinker is now susceptible; sexual desires are aroused and he or she orders another drink and asks a sexy person to dance. Closeness occurs, arousal occurs. The body needs no help, but the spirits impose thoughts and graphic images into the person's mind.

The next step: the sexy person suggests a hotter bar. It is filled with heavier spirits "vibing" each other and its inhabitants. The behavior and standards manifested are those of the spirits and the people given over to them. Relaxed, semi-intoxicated, the person is now in the hands of the spirits; they lead the person as far as he or she will go, into new territory of sexual sin, other drugs (aside from alcohol) and increasing debauchery. Watch out – get free. Just run – but it may be too late, you may be in their clutches and too far down the lust road to stop.

The leading of any spirit works in similar ways. Again, the general operating rules of the spirit world are the same for all spirits. The Holy Spirit works similarly, but with saintly destinations. The Holy Spirit-led person will to go to a worship service, then to meet with some Christians who choose to speak of the things of God. A company of Christians is encountered. Ideas flow: giving to missions, helping someone in need, etc. The person and group move closer to God. The presence of God (versus evil spirits) grows and everyone moves closer to God and engages in further acts that are useful for everyone along the way.

Spirit places

Physical places have a coexisting spirit "place" in the spirit dimension. The physical environment and furnishings reflect something of the spirit environment and "furnishings". The focus here is how the environment affects you so you can choose to avoid a sin/evil provoking environment. Note, however, that placing a mission or church in a sin-filled area has the effect of weakening the evil spiritual environment. There are times (under God's leadership) to enter evil environments with the things and Person of God.

There is also a spirit "place" where our spirits can go even without "out of body" travel or visiting physical lairs. We can mentally and spiritually hang out with spirits through music, meditation, and sharing thoughts and emotions with them. Our stay with them will affect our mind, decisions, and heart. Pornography and its effects are a very good example of this process.

With good reason, the Bible says to bring **every thought** under control. Be careful, watch out.

Spirits inside

As noted earlier, Satan's hope—through every religion, system, philosophy, belief and sin—is to place spirits in you so you're convinced of the truth of their profane doctrine; i.e. his confederate spirits "testify" as to their doctrine and the benefits of their class of sin or life style. Their purpose is to keep you subscribed to their doctrine and to empower and use your body to manifest and experience their sin and drag you to Hell.

Your body is a *vehicle* **designed** to carry spirits: your own and the fullness of God. When the doors are opened to ungodly influences, evil spirits gain entry. Under the right circumstances, it can be as simple for them to gain access to you as it is for you to climb into a car.

Satan has far more success putting spirits inside people (even before birth) than you may be aware. If you have given your heart (or your mind) to a philosophy, religion, occult practice, spirit guide, opened your chakras (allowed a spirit to enter them) or otherwise gone deeply with or into them, or come from a family where these things have taken place, or if you have entered into substantial sin or come from a dysfunctional family and raised inside its culture of unhealthy practices, you are probably feeling the impact of indwelling spirits yourself.

These spirits exert pressure to convince you to do something. The pressure comes from within. In more extreme cases, you may lose control over certain areas of your life. For example, no matter how often you decide not to drink, have sex, etc., you can't stop. In these cases, a spirit acts inside you and has overcome your own will. When the spirit within applies pressure, you succumb to the spirit's wiles and surrender your body to it. In the case of a religious or spiritual belief, a spirit may take over a part of your heart and mind and continually "testify" to the "truth" of what it is trying to get you to believe.

This also occurs within lifestyles. For example, homosexual spirits are, in my opinion, prideful: they declare that what God has called sin to be an acceptable alternative lifestyle. Another example are Marijuana spirits, they also proclaim their doctrine. (Note: many prescription "treatment" drugs are as bad or worse.) Anyone whose mind is controlled by these spirits will believe and proclaim the "party line."

IMPORTANT NOTE: A spirit, or spirits, inside you does not mean you're completely possessed. In most cases, true possession requires many spirits (see Demoniac of Gandara). But it does mean that there are rats in the walls of your body and parts of your understanding. As I said, their thoughts become a sometimes inseparable part of your thoughts. (See Isaiah 65:2b)

When they are in control, you will think and see things the way they want you to think and see them. When they gain additional control, you will also want what they want.

When you accept Jesus, authority over those spirits is given to you. That does not mean you will have control over them immediately, although the authority has been given to you. The exercise of your authority starts when you **renounce the doctrines and other suggestions of ungodly spirits, when you command them to go and release all the "stuff" that has tied them to you. You have the authority to say "no."** This requires a decision of the mind *and* of the heart. (As explained earlier, the heart is where many bondages lie.)

Getting your heart in condition to free it from twisted spirits will take time. Often, there are unexpected elements you'll have to tackle. When your heart is right and you have to cut the ties to the "underworld," you may need the help of another person to cast the spirits out. *But until the places where the spirit lived are covered, healed and filled with God, God's stuff, and yourself, the spirit will often be able to return.*

There is mistaken doctrine in the western Church (although not in poor or heavily demon-oppressed countries where the church consciously and regularly deals with spirits) that a saved person cannot have indwelling demonic spirits. This is categorically not true. In my mission work, I ran across born again, Spirit-filled people *all the time* that needed deliverance from evil spirits.

Something I have observed and lived: when God comes in while strong spirits co-exist with you, they are in part overcome as a result of your new life in God. They may have only a weak influence, but they are still there. In this state, they may lie dormant for years, but when you are weak, or tragedy hits (often because they partially blind you), they will take back some measure of control. Don't hide in denial or insanity. Be aware and fight now. My mother hid in selective insanity (while otherwise functioning); she simply created realities and memories that were fiction to avoid the horror of her life. It is very probable that some of the spirits manifesting in your life entered pre-birth. They came in through generational holes, not through your own sin, and may have made much of your life horrible.

More comments on spirits inside

As mentioned, one of the goals of the spirits is to live through you. They want a body to manifest their desires in the physical so they can enjoy physical pleasure. This fallen world is as it is in large part because of the rebellious spirits which continuously manifest their desires through accessible human beings. By manifesting inside a human body, they gain authority and power in the physical world. <u>Their kingdoms rule.</u> In the process, they make you who they want you to be.

As already noted, their victims (us) share a thought process, *a "virtual reality,"* a life with them. Victim and spirit become one in some area, or areas, of life. Unless the process is turned around, ungodly spirits take control of as much of their victims' life as they can; life (as opposed to Life which is being connected to God is co-opted and shared with them.

Of special note here is that many types of spirits bring pleasure. Sex spirits bring pleasure by manipulating the physical body and the mind. Part of the process of being free is to renounce inappropriate pleasure and invest in pleasure toward God. Sex in itself is not bad (in fact it is a good thing that God made for us to enjoy) if enjoyed within the parameters that God sets.

Prevalent also are spirits of depression. They make as many events as possible look bad: everything is "half empty". If you have to take an antidepressant, consider that you very well may be dealing with a spirit of depression that makes you see and **feel** everything through a depressive shield.

Unlike wicked spirits who want to live inside you to use and destroy you, God wants to live inside you to lead you to, and give you, a new and better life. And just as we all-too-often share life with indwelling twisted spirits and co-participate in their acts, thoughts and emotions, God wants to live in us and for us to share life with Him. **The process is the same for all spirits. The rules are the same.**

Beware death spirits

Remember that Satan, including all of the spirits that follow him and everything of his multitudinous kingdoms and systems, are death (but very real). Death is his nature and signature. Living on this fallen planet surrounded by death can become overwhelming to a point where we no longer care if we live or die. To complicate the issue, when we truly understand Who God is and what He has for us in heaven (a VERY real place), our desire to depart and be with Him can grow.

The problem with not caring about life as it exists right now is that we open ourselves to not taking care of ourselves and, in more developed cases, we invite death spirits into our body and inadvertently open our family (and those under our covering) to them.

Death spirits can go after you when you're with those you love most, exposing them to danger from car wrecks, ship wrecks, airplane crashes, etc. Death spirits can also open you to heart attacks, cancer, and other diseases in which people experience slow torment and death at the devil's hand. There are other types of "death spirits" that bring economic, social, and other kinds of death including "ruin" and destroy some part of your life.

If you have already opened that door, *close it in the name of Jesus*. Say: "In the name of Jesus, I close every window and door of death to me and those under my covering. I renounce and reject every kind of death spirit. I will only die to those things that Jesus wants me to die to. I cut off from me, and from those under my covering, every evil manifestation of death. Jesus, I will die to those things that you want me to die to, so that I may have abundant life."

An additional comment about death: accept no death – neither of life, love, work, friendships, etc. Remember, Jesus came to give life more abundantly.

I have to interject here that there is there is a godly kind of death: death to sin and the sinful nature. Satan promotes death of life, God promotes death to death. Reject Satan's deaths. Embrace God's deaths (to sin, ungodly self)...for they are life and Life.

Masks, lies, acting and identities

The things we're not able to release, forgive, etc. are bound to those parts of our lives that consist of the masks, lies (regarding how we feel and are), roles and identities we live. Fear and hiding are key elements here.

For example, when extremely hurt or rejected, people often wear a mask of being "ok." They lie to themselves and others about their pain by denying it, then they choose a role and act like they don't care. Often, they'll reject their true self and adopt another identity (outlaw biker for example) that essentially broadcasts, "I'm blowing off the whole world."

As an aside, in such cases there is almost certainly unforgiveness toward the offenders, unforgiveness toward oneself for being hurt and rejected, and unforgiveness for actions taken to deny the hurt and/or survive (perhaps drugs, sexual promiscuity, and other ungodly pleasures, etc.).

In assuming a role, an entire identity may be created to try to live a less pain-filled life. I have seen awful "new" lives built over even more horrible "old" lives.

Sadly, this approach, aside from the awful spiritual consequences, only serves to reinforce the original problem; their having to act at all re-affirms the existence of their hurt and little or no healing occurs. In Jesus, we are new people. The key to healing and release is to know God, become the person who He created us to be, and take the life He has for us. Then hiding and acting becomes increasingly irrelevant.

Matters like these can be complicated further by indwelling spirits and spiritual DNA. A person may have inherited a spirit from pre-birth; in the above case, a spirit of rejection (or perhaps a "lone wolf" spirit). When this occurs, at every step in this person's life, the spirit twists information about situations the person is in, creating hurt emotions and faulty conclusions: "This thing happened because I am not accepted; I don't measure up." In addition to the spirits, "spiritual DNA" may exist: deposits of rejection and hurt made of spirit material that are passed to the child from his/her parents and/or accumulated during life.

The unraveling of this mess requires the ongoing help of the Holy Spirit but starts with **forgiving yourself and others and releasing your own life and its ways**. (The compounded presence of the Holy Spirit through baptism in the Holy Spirit is perhaps essential as well.) There is no other way than to sit in the presence of a godly therapist (not all are competent in this area) and/or with the Holy Spirit and get to the *core of the hurt*. Hurt people have to deal with the *reality* of the hurt, the pain and the lies (versus the insane denial of them). They have to go deep and *work at forgiving* (themselves and others) and deal with the emotions that are exposed. Crying, anger, despair, and pain will occur. As they do, God must be invited into every millimeter of your being and life. God's presence in these sealed off areas (as well as in all areas) brings healing and life. He is healing. He is life.

To make matters worse, in many cases a damaged person will have allowed an ungodly spirit to take over certain functions of his or her life. In these instances, the *real person is hiding behind a demon* (this is common in shy and/or rejected persons), creating an extremely unhealthy symbiotic relationship: the person accepts (whether knowingly or not) the demon "persona" to hide behind and the demon gets a human body to live out its desires. In many cases the evil spirit will emanate reactions that are acceptable only to similarly-infested people (kindred spirits). The result: the victim becomes locked in the pain, or some variation of it, while living in a type of fantasy.

An outlaw biker or pirate is a good example of a fantasy life constructed atop piles of unacknowledged pain and rejection. In a sense, fantasy is a lesser degree of insanity. When the pain gets too great, some people will allow a spirit of insanity to enter and fantasy will become insanity. Fantasy and insanity are logical (and in a sense, sane) alternatives to a painful world and existence but they are horrible choices and, once made, it's hard to take control over them and their corresponding spirits and spirit stuff. Even excessive romanticism is a type of fantasy.

Separation from the masks, lies, roles, and identities (and the spirits involved) is a massive undertaking, but it's the only way to freedom. **One must decide to *face the truth, the hurt and pain*; one must choose to forgive the hurt, ask God into every part of it and all the resulting mess; one must give up the lies and identities and become what we really are: children of God through Jesus Christ.** *It has to be enough to be one of God's kids*, to be his son or daughter, to renounce the wrong impartation of family, identity, pleasures and ambitions and look to God as Father and become like him. Incidentally, as we become what we really are, we leave behind the old person who suffered/created the problem(s). In my opinion, to be willing to do this, we have to understand who God is and that we **can** be complete in Him. His personality is more than big enough for us to find a place of comfort in Him while being His *and* ourselves. He is not boring, limited, or unimaginative – nor are we in Him.

The process of becoming one of God's kids and discovering our identity and purpose in Him is something the Father does (or tries to do) in the lives of everyone who comes to Him through Jesus. The process is much deeper in people with mangled lives and hearts. Hurt people have to leave their carefully constructed and constrained lives so they can venture out to become God's beloved child. The wonderful thing is that being God's kid is MUCH better than anything else, so there is no real loss; only the loss of a life that didn't work. (See the section on the nature and personality of God.)

Related to masks, lies, identities, and roles are the attitudes, thoughts, opinions, illnesses, limitations, hardheartedness, aggressions, flirtations and "f--- you" (instead of loving) attitudes that we surround ourselves with to protect ourselves. We can lose these, too, when we recognize and embrace our identity in God.

To be who God created you to be and to be happy you have to give up the ungodly thoughts, things and activities that made you attractive and successful in your present life. That may go to the very core of your present identity. Big issue: do you trust God to give you a good, better and happy new self in exchange for what you have now? If you're in serious pain or torment so that the pleasure given is less than the torment, and if you are willing to deal with the hurts and addictions, your answer may be "yes." If not, you'll likely continue to manifest the desires of another spirit or spirits even in your Christian life.

Further release: Giving stuff to God

There are many traps and habits that most of us deal with at one time or another. Although giving stuff to God is linked to renunciation (often the first step), there is an ongoing process and defense of "giving stuff to God." I've had to give alcohol to God forever.

There will be times when God quickens you to give something to him forever, or to give a specific thing to him for a time to take it out of you so you can withstand an imminent or approaching temptation. For example, God may request that you give violence to Him to protect you from a situation that will arise. And because violence gets relinquished to God, you will refuse to get into a fight that otherwise would have caused unpremeditated injuries or death.

Giving stuff to God is a key to your freedom. It is also the ongoing work of God in your life; it should comfort you that He is with you.

Cutting things off

Regarding spiritual connections such as the threads created

through sexual relationships and lust (and many other ways), they are *very real things in the spirit world.* They continue to entangle and cripple their victims until they are cut off. I have had to sit alone in the presence of God and cut spirit ties while renouncing ungodly relationships (and desires and ambitions). I do this by saying, "In the name of Jesus Christ I cut off the spirit, sex and soul ties with_____."

Taking things off

The apostle Paul says to take off things—even the unredeemed man. I have found it useful to take off lust, anger, unforgiveness, and other things with my hands as I renounce them with my mouth. For example, I say: "I take off anger." With my hands, I make motions as though I am taking off a sweater and I give it to God, or at times I just throw it down to the ground. In my experience, taking things off is a tool that God has given us.

Closing windows and doors

Like the natural world, the spirit world has windows and doors. (Rev. 4:1). God can open these windows and doors for us. A personal prophecy, word or scripture from God often discloses a window through which we can "see" something He wants to reveal to us.

The focus of this section, though, is the windows and doors

through which demons have access to you. In a perfect world (sinless), your ancestors and parents would never have opened unholy doors to you, so alcoholism (as just one example) would not come from your ancestors. Note alcoholism, like depression, lust, etc. run in families because of this principle.

It is through such doors (whether generational or self opened through your actions) that certain spirits and spirit "stuff" gain access to you. **Assuming that a particular spirit does not inhabit your body, access by the spirit and its stuff can be cut off by closing the door or window that allows the access. Even when a spirit does inhabit your body, closing access still places a kind of barrier between the person and the spirits.**

The process begins (and, in some cases, may end) by saying, "In the name of Christ Jesus, I close the windows and doors of alcoholism (using alcohol as an example) to _____ (your name and/or the name of another person)."

Other work may have to be done, so it may be appropriate to add, "In the name of Christ Jesus, I cut every soul, spirit and body tie between _____ (your name and/or the name of another person) and alcohol."

By the way, if you're interceding on another's behalf, this type of ministry doesn't require his or her presence or consent. It initiates a process that brings the person to a place where he or she can finally decide, freely, what course to take. When people are in bondage, they aren't free to do so; they're a slave to that which has overpowered them.

A most memorable experience was the case of the 13 year old daughter of a friend. I could see that there was something wrong in the way she acted toward men. I asked God about it. He told me there was an open door of perversion in her life. I said, "In the name of Jesus I close the door of perversion to _____." The next time I saw her, she was a different person entirely. It was as if she had received a brain transplant. Often the Lord has quickened me to re-close that door to her.

Trauma holes and other types of holes

Related to windows and doors are holes. A spiritual hole resembles a hole in the line of scrimmage through which an opposing team can sack a quarterback in American football. Just as doors and windows can be closed, holes can be closed, but they can also be covered or filled in.

Much of what I shared in the section about lies, masks, and identities is due to access that the enemy has to people through doors, windows or holes. Doors, as you recall, may have been opened by ancestors; the lies, masks, and identities people use are often efforts to deal with those consequences. We, too, can open doors—for good or for evil—and elect to wear the lies, masks and identities that come with them. Upon understanding the process we can choose to relinquish the "stuff" that entered and our reactions to it for something better, something eternally blessed: our own true life/Life.

Although the ways doors and holes affect us are similar, holes are different in nature. God created us to be covered. When we're younger, we're supposed to have the covering of family. (Sadly, in this fallen world, this doesn't always happen adequately; sometimes not at all.) At work, we're supposed to have the covering of more experienced people so we keep from making dangerous mistakes. Without covering, we find ourselves dealing with things we aren't equipped to handle.

A hole is an open space in life's line of scrimmage through which spirits and ungodly things have access to us. Through them, we experience things we're not ready to tackle because of inexperience or lack of strength. For a child, lack of covering can result in multiple tragedies from death itself to depravity (often sexual). Losing our cover (or not having it) can also cause us to relinquish the weapons God has given us. The hole in the line of scrimmage allows you to be "sacked" (American football).

Love is the most important covering. A truly loved person feels secure, (barring other problems, generational spirits, etc.) and will be covered in many ways. Such a person is protected and in a position to make wise and safe decisions and to reject much temptation. Loved people know their worth to others and to themselves. This is why one of the key things devils do is to try to keep humans from understanding the immense love of God, and it is why God's command to us is to love. **The love of God and of other people prevents damage and also helps repair the damage caused by any prior lack of covering. Love also gives us the desire and courage to go on.**

There are times when a hole is so large that only God can cover and eventually fill it. In these cases, often caused by a trauma of some kind, only God can provide the necessary profound love and other resources. This is especially true in the case of a broken heart. A broken heart results in a huge hole in our covering. That hole in your covering allows satanic access and may drive you to unhealthy behaviors and substitutes. There are additional reasons why people are driven into the ditch, but a broken heart is a major cause.

God acts directly to heal trauma by **faithfully** pouring Himself and His love into individuals. In Luke 4:18, Jesus said, reading from the book of the prophet Isaiah, "The Spirit of the Lord is upon Me, Because He has anointed Me to preach the Gospel (Good News) to the poor, He has sent Me to heal the brokenhearted, To preach deliverance to the captives, And recovery of sight to the blind, To set at liberty those who are oppressed...." Jesus came to fill the trauma holes and to heal. His Presence is covering and healing.

You and I also are part of God's resources. God wants to use us to manifest love to other people in need of His providence. We are commanded to love, to cover people when required (gently), and to refill ourselves with His love so we can be effective.

Self love

The Bible says that we are to love others as we love ourselves. Repeat for emphasis: *...as we love ourselves*. You can help fill and cover the holes in your own life by loving yourself *even as you hate your sin*. Be kind to yourself. Be kind to others, too.

Heartbreak / broken hearts

Heartbreak is awful. It was never part of God's plan. As I explained, death and all other evil entered because of man's choice to know good and evil. When man chose to know good and evil, the door to the Evil One opened at humankind's behest. So in that sense, all heartbreak (a form of evil) comes from the Evil One. It is part of his evilness and his kingdoms.

That said, not all heartbreak comes *directly* from the devil's hand. The death of a loved one, the loss of relationship with someone you love, sickness, etc, are often the immediate cause of heartbreak without the devil acting in a specific way in the particular event. But in many cases he has, and is, acting, and your heartbreak is simply the fruition of his hidden, long-term plan for your life. Regardless of cause, heartbreak is real. <u>The world is full of broken hearts and heartbreak</u>. Heaven and our future in God will be utterly free from it.

God was and is aware of heartbreak: His own for the loss of creation and His loss of so many people to their own way. He is also aware of our heartbreak. He feels it. Jesus came to open the door of relationship with God the Father so He could heal the brokenhearted (Is. 61:1).

<u>Heartbreak is so devastating that people can, and very often do, die of it, rapidly or slowly</u>, sometimes through alcohol or overeating. **During times of heartbreak, God can and does help us.** He lives in our hearts and His Presence can and does heal them. In the heartbreak process (which I know all too well through the death of certain life dreams, the loss of a marriage, and the death of my wife in an automobile accident), it is often only (or mostly) God who pulls us through. Initially, **He may act by placing us into a different, best possible available situation to keep us alive; He may give us work or daily activities to do to be sure we put one foot in front of the other until we realize we'll survive and learn to thrive again; and/or He'll take whatever other steps are necessary to deal with us as individuals.**

The key thing to know is that in our helplessness, He will provide a way forward so that as time passes He can heal us. Even in heartbreak, however, God expects us to do what we can, as much or as little as that may be. Action is what God expects/ requires of us. Applying the principles you find here will expedite your recovery if your heart is broken. One day a new view of life will be visible, a new plan will seem possible, then a new course, until one day a bit of happiness and joy will return to you. In the fullness, He will give you the promised abundant life.

Loneliness

A comment about loneliness: for those of us who have lived for decades in this fallen world and suffered the consequences, there is often emptiness, a sense of failure, a feeling of shame and hurt at the core of our beings. Many times the cause is because at key points in our lives our family and/or friends failed to teach us, affirm us and be there for and with us. These vacant places ache to be filled from bottom to top. Because of this, loneliness drives and can foster sin. Not that we want to sin; we want real love, companionship, we want to be useful, and we want to fill the chasm of loneliness and emptiness. The sense of loneliness can be so horrible that we'll try almost **anything** to escape it or to correct it.

If that is your situation, know that God wants to enter and heal your core. It will require work and your decision to <u>trust</u> in God. **If your trauma is immense, someone may have to help you, but know that God has resources. My experience is that**

if you're willing to accept help, God will provide what and who you need. If you don't already see the provision, ask God to open your eyes to what He is doing. In your battle with loneliness, know and claim that in truth *__you are not alone: God is with you always.__*

Making the decision to go on

Your circumstances may be so difficult that you don't want to go on; options include disability, bitterness, anger, isolation, death, suicide and just giving up. An early gateway to receiving more life is to make the decision to move forward *__no matter how wounded or tired you may be.__* And if you are so down that you can't make the decision to "go on" all the time, make it when you can.

Part of the process of moving on is to do the things I've outlined in this book. But doing everything you find here will only be partially successful unless you give up ungodly "escapes." There all kinds of "escapes", including those mentioned above and drugs of all kinds (valium, cocaine, meth, alcohol, etc.) and sex, perversion, violence, hate, etc. *In Jesus alone you can go on with life, and in Jesus you can deal with fear and trauma.* Jesus is enough to satisfy the real needs that drive a person to ungodly escape and death. Escaping into unhealthy activities is never the answer. Escaping into intellectualism and insanity is not the answer. The answer is to go on, with and into God, and to do in the natural and spirit areas whatever is necessary. Ultimately, I believe <u>you have to come to a point of believing and trusting that God alone is enough and that He will provide what you need *and go into it with you*</u>. The achieving of trusting God is a process between you and God. <u>Just don't quit!</u>

Escape into praise and God

God has given us an escape, a "place" where we can be protected. It's praising God. As the enemy works to overtake us with fear, despair, doubt, and thought hooks to drag us into danger and sin, praising God is part of the way out of danger.

The Bible shows us the importance of praise for withstanding the enemy and receiving from God. Judah (the son of Jacob) means PRAISE. Of all the tribes of Israel, the tribe of Judah remained in the Promised Land longest and was principal in its restoration. Jesus was a descendant of Judah and is referred to as the Lion of the tribe of Judah; that is, the Lion (King and Lord) of the tribe of Praise. In fact, it may be said that Jesus is the leader of Praise. He continually leads us in praising God the Father if we're able to hear Him. The last Psalms (144 – 150) are all songs of praise to God.

I have lived the importance of Praise. Praise in my life allows me to refocus on God. Praise overcomes the worries and fears and cuts off the enemy. When I praise God, I see things differently: my perception of "reality" changes and I can see things as they are for me in God.

This is best illustrated by one of the few night vision dreams I've received from God. In the dream, I was walking along a road with high walls on both sides. As I approached an intersection I looked to the left and right. In both directions the road was the same: paved, clean and with a high wall on each side. I had little choice; no matter where I walked, I was walled inside a sterile landscape. In my dream, as soon as I began to praise God, suddenly the walls disappeared and I found myself in a green, grassy field with pleasant vegetation and a 360 degree view. All possibilities existed; every direction was open to me. Through praise, I escaped limited possibilities and walked easily into a verdant land and endless horizons.

Praising God is an important tool in your bag of spiritual weapons. It will help you combat despair, help expand your vision, and carry you into God's presence.

The Bible says that God inhabits the praise of His people. Use it. Revel in it. **Praise God in all things. No matter what is happening, praising God will protect you and give you a different perspective.** Often when I missed Maggie (my late wife) God prompted me to thank Him that she was (and is) safe and well with Him. Those words changed how I thought and felt about her death: even today they make me glad that she is safe, well and happy. She is there and we will see each other at the right time.

Claiming God's provision and the things of God

God has declared certain provisions in the Bible: He has given us authority over our own lives and over spirits, things of the world, and certain earthly matters to combat Satan as he comes to steal, kill and destroy.

In your life, claim the fact that you are dead to sin. That does not mean that you don't sin, but that your sin-loving self has died and after you sin you know it is wrong and begin to hate it. Claiming the fact that you are "dead to sin" will help in times of temptation and even as you give in to the sin; claiming that you are dead to sin will limit your participation. Claim also that you are a new creation in Christ and that the old man has died with Christ on the cross. These are useful tools and will grow in their effectiveness the more you use them. Use them when you need them the most: while struggling with sin, even awful sin. Stay with yourself, God stays with you. Do your part, use the tools.

In the area of other provisions (job, love, joy, etc.), God gives us what we need and more. The devil does not want us to receive or keep them and will steal them whenever he can. When that happens, **claim them**. You have the authority to do so, *and the devil knows it*. (The question is: ***Do you***?) Beware, the devil will try to keep you from exercising your authority by disparaging the act of naming what God has provided and claiming it from the devil. Sometimes we have the ability to see what the devil is doing; at other times we'll be guessing. In either case, if there is something good that you want or need (and it doesn't require that you or God overcome someone else's <u>free</u> will), claim it.

For example: you can afford a new house, you have chosen it carefully, but the deal seems to be escaping you. **Claim it!** Say: "In the name of Christ Jesus, I claim the house."

Regarding the will of another: there are times when he or she cannot make a <u>free will</u> choice because of spiritual (demonic) oppression. In this case, you may be able to claim something for the person because you are not violating his or her *free* will. (For example, claim freedom from a habit or habits for that person.)

Using the name of Jesus Christ of Nazareth

Please Note: in this book, the name of Jesus identifies the name of the God we call upon or in whose name we act. *Not all people invoking the name of Jesus are calling on God.* In the Spanish culture, many people are named Jesus. The Jesus of the Bible is the Second Person of God Almighty – forever alive, forever God, not part of any creation. There are also so-called Christian sects that don't call upon the Jesus of the Bible (their Jesus was created by Father God). The same with New Age worshippers: the "Christ Spirit" is not the Jesus of the Bible.

That said, using **the Name of Jesus, i.e. - calling upon God Almighty, is the most powerful name you or I**

can use (Philippians 2:9). Through the use of the Name, we acknowledge God Almighty and we place ourselves within the plan of salvation, acknowledging our sin, our need for a Savior, and identify ourselves as beneficiaries of what Christ did through His death.

It is virtually always useful to use Jesus' name. Just His Name, with no other prayer or word, is powerful. It is both a tool and a weapon. It cuts to the core of every spiritual issue with power. Use it alone, use it in prayer, use it to claim God's provision for you and your family, use it to claim the things outlined in this book and use it against the devil – for it is by and through His name and what it stands for that we have authority.

One time I was witnessing on a street in Seattle, Washington. I found a man hunched over in a semi-comatose state, dressed in an old overcoat, reeking of urine. I walked over to him and said, "Just say the name of Jesus, Jesus, Jesus, Jesus, Jesus, Jesus." The man stood straight up and, with clarity and obvious intelligence, barked at me, "By what authority do you use The Name?"

The name of Jesus had cut through to the core of the spirits possessing the man and, in an effort to stop the torment caused them by the Name, they asked me by whose authority I was disturbing them. I succeeded at what I intended. The message was clear to the man inside the body: the Name was powerful and useful to him.

Few uses of the Name of Jesus are as instantly dramatic or graphic as what occurred with that man, but in the spirit world the Name is working. The effect is there. Evil spirits are rocked back on their heels. We are given Jesus' name to use at will (for good, not for swearing!). I use it all the time.

Binding devils / exorcism and deliverance

Yeah, exorcism is real, but everything at the right time. This book is about how to receive and live the abundant life that Jesus promises. <u>An inseparable part of the abundant life is accepting the new personhood that God has for you</u>. Until you or someone else is ready to be the new person, deliverance (exorcism) will not work – or if it does, the spirits will simply return. Deliverance is usually a process.

Having said this, there are times to use the name of Jesus to tie up (bind) the spirits with the spirit bonds (think ropes) created by your words and to cast the spirits out of a person by using your faith, authority, and the supernatural power you've been given.

I often bind (tie up spirits) that are harassing or working against people and nations. As an example of how I do this for my family, I say "I bind you, Satan, from my children, grandchildren and descendants and all those married into them. I include my spiritual descendants."

I also pray for them, asking God to bless them, protect them, and work in them so that there is always more Jesus in them and their lives.

When confronted with a person who is tormented or when a spirit has taken over a body so that the body looks like the spirit and not the human, I will say, "I bind you, Satan, and I command you to come out of him or her." I have seen some dramatic demonic possessions: I have seen fingers grow and form four knuckles. I have seen faces form into gargoyle faces as the spirits manifest under the skin and control it. All fallen spirits are ugly (they are disconnected from God and deteriorating) when seen as they really are. They only masquerade as pretty spirits of light. Casting out spirits is real, but seek God on the timing.

We are dealing with spirits almost constantly and there are ministries specifically anointed to free extremely demonically tormented or possessed individuals. Although not dangerous, it is much more effective to work with people who are experienced in and anointed for that type of ministry.

Dressing self with Christ, His blood, and our new self

Renunciation, release, cutting stuff off, closing windows and doors, giving stuff to God, etc. are part of the process of getting free. We are told to "take off the old man (or woman)" and all associated with him/her: death, immorality, lust, anger, division, violence, greed, idolatry, etc. **The other part is to put Christ on, to dress ourselves with Him. The baptism of the Holy Spirit is yet another part, covering ourselves with God.**

In the case of Christ, I suggest that you literally say and <u>perform with your hands</u> the taking off of your old self and putting on of Christ. Use your hands to "take off" the old self (like a garment), then "put Christ on". As I "put Christ on", I say "I wash myself with the blood of Jesus Christ and dress myself with the life and person of Jesus Christ." The Bible teaches that we are forgiven only though Jesus' blood. Being bathed in His blood cleanses us and allows God to be "on" and in us. The Bible also teaches that life is in the blood. By dressing ourselves with Jesus' blood, we are dressing ourselves with Life.

Making right choices

Nothing in this teaching excuses you from making all the godly choices you <u>can</u> (see Proverbs). If you choose sin, the desires of the flesh (and the other wrong stuff) will grow in your life. If you're a slave to them, or fall (again), but want to do right, then God's grace will keep you in Him while you use the tools of God to get free. The effect of the tools taught here may be great or small, but the tools are at work for you. In your struggles against sin, look at the Ten Commandments and the letters of the New Testament as easy guides for right actions in God's sight.

Wisdom (and more right choices)

Wisdom is knowing how to do things (in ways approved by God) to be successful. If you want economic prosperity, in most cases you'll have to study, train, work hard, submit to the boss and spend money wisely. If you want health and a strong body, you'll have to eat well, exercise, avoid substances that damage you *and* claim the promises of God regarding healing.

Wisdom is also about knowing the time and place to do things (including speaking out). There is a time and place for everything; part of wisdom is discerning the correct time and place. The Book of Proverbs is a good place to meditate on what to do and how. It is also wise to ask God how to do things. The Bible says in James 1:5–8 that God desires to tell and teach us how to do things. Ask Him, then believe what He says.

Planting and reaping

The Word of God is a seed; you have to plant it in good soil. In the same way an earthly seed will produce according to its nature, so it is with spiritual seed. In an earthly garden, you plant, water and care for the seed; you must do the same with spiritual seed. So plant the seed, declare it, do whatever is necessary along the way, and care for the plant that grows from the Word. It *will* take time for the seed you plant to grow, and more seed may need to be planted; your key is to continue planting, watering, and caring for the seed. You need to do this whether or not you see results at the time you think you should. (God promises that the plant will eventually sprout and grow if you remain constant regarding its care.)

The concept of planting and reaping applies to every kind of seed (good and bad, so watch what you plant!) and every part of your life. Your focus here is *planting, and caring for* the planting of the Word of God: the words of the Bible and God's words spoken directly into your life that have been confirmed as truly coming from Him.

The above principle is relevant to all aspects of your life. For example, God says you are to plant good seeds in all areas of your earthly life; spiritual, family, work, social, etc. In work, you train, arrive on time, show respect, and work hard. These are seeds and will produce a good work environment for you over time. In your social life, you show kindness, love, spend time, share experiences, etc. Over time, the fruit of these exchanges (seeds) will grow and produce fruit: you'll eventually become part of a community.

In all areas of your life, be careful to choose what you want your life to look like in the future. Plant the seed you want to see thriving in the future; it will become your future *reality*. If you don't know what you want your life to look like, plant the things of God – He'll script your life.

Cautionary Note about the universality of this physical and

spiritual rule: If you plant pornography, or other bad seed, it will grow and produce fruit according to its kind. (If you have done that, rip it out of the ground with the words: "I rip out all the bad seed and plants that I have planted. I destroy them in the name of Jesus.")

Weavings

As mentioned in the first section of this book, there is a "spiritual fabric" to our lives. We literally are woven into a spiritual fabric. This fabric exists prior to our birth. We are born into the fabric of our families, our ancestors, and their spiritual lives. What happens to us, and our own actions, further sew us into that fabric and creates new fabric (good or bad). Once we accept Jesus and understand good and evil and how the spirit dimension works, we can start consciously affecting the weave and begin weaving a new life, freeing ourselves from the undesirable parts of the old.

To expedite this process, it is useful to undo the old fabric with our words. I do it this way; I say "In the name of Christ Jesus (or Jesus Christ) I rip apart the ungodly and un-useful fabric of my life and I speak and create a new fabric through and in Jesus Christ."

Dream weavings

Another source of weavings is dreams. In my experience,

dreams are seldom self-generated, but are spirit communications (rarely from God) to our semi-conscious minds. Remember, spirits "talk" through inserting thoughts into your mind and spirit. A clear example of dream weaving by spirits occurred to a woman I know. She was happy with her boyfriend, but over years had reoccurring dreams of herself with another woman. Finally, she decided to try lesbianism. She now lives with her girlfriend. She was dream woven into a life over the years by fallen (evil) spirits. She accepted the dreams (weavings) and was sewn into the life they designed.

Note, in the example above, to excuse the dreams as coming from God you have to totally disregard the Old and New Testament prohibitions on homosexuality.

If you are being woven into a reality through dreams, you can reject them and destroy the weavings in the name of Jesus Christ.

Trusting God

The very nature of our existence – *small conscious specks on the decaying open surface of a molten ball covered by a thin layer of solidified material, lightly protected by a thin atmosphere, hurtling through space at terrific speed and open to the cosmos* – is enough to make a person insane. You and I, with an understanding of creation, stare into the universe. The words that come to mind are: **magnificent and fragile.**

Our precarious existence (outside of God) on this planet, together with the continuous onslaught of evil (including loss, sadness, and all issues mentioned herein), the free will of others (which God does not always interfere with), residing in a body with a fallen nature that desires sin, living the fruit of bad seed we and others have planted (perhaps in total ignorance), and generally just living in this fallen world which is being judged and condemned by God...*make it hard to trust God.*

Due to the above and for all the reasons explained in this book, life can be, often *is*, very difficult and/or very discouraging, with struggles aplenty and bad things happening to good people. God's people seem to suffer the same diseases and other problems that unbelievers and followers of other gods endure. (see Ecclesiastes 8:14, and 9:11 & 12).

There are answers. I've dealt with some of them in this book. There are principles that you, as loved by God, can apply to live better, conquer infirmity and be protected. But know this: life in a fallen world is what we're saddled with. You will lose battles. You will be ambushed. You aren't immune...you don't escape the battles. But trusting in the goodness and justice of God is your strongest defense against panicky reactions, wrong decisions, despair, hopelessness, fear, worry and "running." Christians of all stripes will act (or fail to act) and will struggle at times under the oppression of depression, fear, perhaps even mental illness because we do not (or sometimes cannot) trust

God. And distrusting God is a horrible thing because of the many dangers it opens up to us.

Even when we decide to trust God, there's the issue of deciding in which areas we should wait for God and trust Him and in which areas we're called to act upon. It is often next to impossible to discern what parts God should do and what parts we should do.

It is hard. My answer: Start by asking God into everything! Leave nothing out, including your sin. Invite him into everything… good *and* bad. (Don't suffer under the delusion that He'll be shocked; He already knows all about your *bads.)*

Pray for God to guide you. Ask Him what things you must handle and what He will do. Ask Him to control events, then make wise decisions based on where you are in your walk with Him (your level of faith, experience and wisdom) and go forward with these words in your mind and on your lips: "I trust You Lord, God of the Bible" or "I trust you, Father God" or "I trust you, Jesus." All mean the same thing; choose the one that feels best to you. **And regardless of what happens, good or bad, whether it goes as you want or not, do not falter in telling God that you trust Him.** When you do, additional trust in God will enter into your entire being and across time joy will show itself, peace will come, and the oppressing spirits will be neutralized.

If you just *can't* trust God for whatever reason (upbringing, wounding, a sense of betrayal, etc.), you exist in a dangerous spiritual reality. <u>In that event, tell someone to pray **_for you_** that you will be able to trust God.</u>

And don't be afraid to tell God you don't trust Him! Ask Him to **_give you_** trust for Him. Talk to God about it. Tell Him everything you think and feel. If you're mad, hurt, angry at Him, TELL HIM. If you think He's failed you, tell Him. Talk to Him. Yell at God. Open a dialogue with your monologue. It **_is_** all about relationship with Him, so go after one! He already knows everything you feel and think: every attitude and blunder hidden in your heart. **By talking to Him about everything, you put it out in the open, put it on the table so the two of you can deal with it.**

But in all this -- try to trust God at **_the highest level you can_**. Say it;__claim__ trusting God. **<u>Make the best decisions you can and trust Him with the rest.</u>** Trusting God will reduce or eliminate trauma and allow Him to bring the best results into your present and future.

Weakness

If you're physically or emotionally unwell, latent spirit "things," spirits, and physical diseases will try to manifest in your life. Even past acts and temptations which have been easily resisted before may rise to the surface to vex you. Drugs (including some prescription drugs, alcohol, and in some cases, caffeine), wrong food, lack of exercise -- *all weaken you.* These factors compound the difficulties; they don't help you. **In whatever measure you can, take care of yourself in all ways. Avoid all recreational drugs and any excess (or maybe even regular use) of alcohol. To some extent your success in receiving God's abundant life will depend on your strength. Using the tools given in this book, build strength wherever you can.**

Addictions

An addiction is anything that you don't want to do (or may even want to do in some way) that you can't stop doing. Addiction is marked by resolutions "never to do it again" – but you do. Whether it's alcohol, violence, abuse, anger, thievery, illegal or prescribed drugs, lust, pornography, adultery, homosexuality, sex, masturbation or something else (even so called "healthy activities") – addiction is *any* behavior that overcomes you or into which you typically "escape reality" for a time.

Addictions often attach slowly; they seem semi-controllable until one day they take over. The months or years of logic, information and learned behavior (habit formation) can make sense (or seem good) even though the Bible says that the activity/ thought is sin. You end up doing things you never thought you would. You know better. You *want* to stop...but you are stuck.

Once the activity or thought is strong there is probably an indwelling spirit that takes temporary control. That spirit can make the addiction extremely pleasurable and when in control is like a second self that you willingly go along with until temporary satisfaction occurs.

Addictions are awful. They pull you, drive you, and ultimately ruin you – your work, your reputation, your family and your life. "Hell and destruction are never full." (Proverbs 20:25) The moment you recognize an addiction, you've taken a crucial step. Don't let shame keep you trapped. God still loves you **and will help you**, but you must take some steps. You can't overcome an addiction alone. You have to get help. The devil does not want us to exercise godly authority or get good things while in this world.

Getting help

If you need help (and if you're dealing with an addiction, you do need help), get it. Don't allow profane spirits to condemn you into remaining alone in your struggle (whether the struggle is an addiction or anything else). The Bible says "For all have sinned and fall short of the glory of God" Roman 3:23. You're not the only one struggling with sin. God will stay with you in your struggle. Part of *trusting* God is *acting in faith* with the understanding that He cares, that He wants to help, and that He has made provision for you. He wants you to get the help you need. Know that *He is the ultimate source of whatever godly help you access.*

There are a couple of important aspects to seeking help. You'll need someone, or multiple people, to help carry the load and guide you. The Bible say, "…confess your trespasses (sins) one to another…." James 5:16. Getting help through God's people is yet another act of faith. You are justified through your faith. Romans 5:1. As you act, let hope of being free from your addiction grow. Paul in Romans 5:5 says that hope (through faith in God) does not disappoint. Getting help is also part of humility and repentance, both of which please God's socks off. **God will bless you just for getting help**!

God has many provisions for help. They include (but are in no way limited to) Celebrate Recovery (for addictions and hang-ups, etc.), Prodigals (for pornography), and Sexoholics Anonymous. Alcoholics Anonymous is good, but has led too many away from forming a relationship with God, so be aware of this if AA is the source you choose; m*ake sure that the Jesus of the Bible is your "higher power."* God offers other provisions, including books, counselors, godly advice, for other problems. If you can't find victory over your problems, ask God where to find help.

When I was still relatively inexperienced in the Lord, I well remember a casual Christian friend whose son went to the

Christian school of which I was a director. He told me he had just completed an alcohol treatment program. He went on to explain that he had been addicted. I remember being somewhat shocked. How could this Christian man have allowed himself to become an alcoholic?! What I didn't realize is that he had been overcome.

Although I was shocked, God wasn't. When the gentleman completed the alcohol program, God renewed him: gave him a new life, a new wife, and a new job. The man had recognized his problem, sought help, and *kept at it until he was freed...* and God blessed him! God never once deserted him in his need; He helped him and returned the sanity he desired. Proverbs 27:15 says, in essence, that when the chaff or hay is cleared away, the new grass can be seen. When you've overcome your struggles, you'll see the tender new blessings that God has for you.

Note: when you first enter a recovery group you may feel weird and sad that you have gotten to this point. Don't dwell on your feelings; enter the group. God loves you and is making a provision for you to be healed.

Becoming strong

Satan will take every good thing from your life if you're unprotected, weak or untrained. If you're strong in the Lord (or someone is strong for you and covering you), you'll remain safe.

You gather strength by understanding and being

aware of your environment, giving your will to God and doing what He says. You gain strength using the weapons, tools (many of them are outlined in this book) and wisdom that God provides to you. God is leading and teaching you so can defend yourself.

When you're weak, Satan --reaching you in the ways shared in this book -- will take whatever is yours, whatever you desire, and render you miserable to whatever extent he can. The Bible says, "When a strong man, fully armed, guards his own palace (life), his goods (life, job, family, love, social life, etc.) are in peace. But when a stronger than he comes upon him and overcomes him, he takes from him all his armor in which he trusted and divides the spoils." Luke 11:21 & 22. You must be strong through the Lord so that Satan will not overwhelm you.

Becoming strong is a **process. At the beginning, God will try to place you in a safe place to protect you. Accept God's provision, whether it seems good to you or not. He will also quickly teach you what you need to know. Use it.** As time goes by, there will be less protection (covering); he will expect you to begin the process of becoming a strong man or woman. Use everything he teaches you along the way. Each phase will be different; trust that God is in control. (Much of the book you hold in your hands reveals how to become strong *through and in God.*)

Fasting – the nuclear bomb in God's arsenal

Water Fasts

Water fasting consists of ingesting nothing but water. It is the nuclear bomb of spiritual tools. When you find yourself in overwhelming temptation, grief, anxiety, condemnation, in need of direction from God, a distressing situation, or when directed by the Lord, engage in a water fast.

Don't over-think this point (there's no mystery or great theory involved). In all my fasting, I have never suffered physical harm (nonetheless, if you have health issues or other issues that you are concerned about, consult your doctor). Fasting takes a decision, <u>will power</u> and lots of water to fill your stomach to help control your hunger. I find that on a three day fast I can continue my normal level of activities, even running until the third day. After that, running makes me tired so I just walk a lot. On a seven day water only fast, I can work and continue my normal activities – I just feel tired and rest more during the last few days; otherwise I'm not limited. I'm 6'1" tall and weigh 170 pounds, so I have very few reserves. I know of one case of a heavier person (and pre-fast a very sick person) who was running long distances by the end of a 40-day water-only fast. So how you feel during your fast will vary.

There have been two occasions I was told to fast to resist something horrendous and unknown to me that lay ahead. These were extreme cases; both times, God helped dramatically. On the first occasion, I couldn't think of a thing I wanted to eat. On the second occasion—with food in my mouth—God caused my throat to hurt so much that I had to spit it out. It was like fire to my throat. I was on an airplane and everyone around me was eating, so I fell to the temptation to eat. Don't count on such dramatic help while on most fasts, but in cases of extreme need God does help continue the fast.

On one of the occasions mentioned above, because of the fast, I was prevented from killing someone who had taken a dream from me and with whom I was very angry. When the situation arose, I could feel my entire being pushed to violence, but I was able to resist. Instead of beating the person, we went out and had a great evening together. On, or after, all fasts, God communicated something important to me, although much less dramatic than on these two occasions.

More on fasting

Other types of fasting are useful as well. There are all day fasts (until evening), juice fasts, and more. Do what you can, but **obey God if He calls you to a specific fast**.

Don't wait for God to tell you to fast. Use this tool whenever you need it. Drink water often to combat the hunger and remain hydrated. The amazing thing is that after various fasts, you will discover *how little you actually need to eat*! In fact, you may find that you feel better NOT EATING; this is the case with me. When I fast often, I'm always surprised to discover that it's BETTER not to eat! Eating clogs up our bodies and spirits.

In my opinion, the mechanism of fasting is that it weakens your flesh, strengthens your will, focuses you on God (if you so choose), and lifts up the spirit man or woman inside (who we *really* are; the spirit person inside the temporary body). Fasting also clears out the toxins in your body that interfere with your spirit. Through the process, fasting helps you better perceive the spirit world and get deeper into God, although on occasion if fasting is very hard for you, you may not experience closeness to God or hear Him or see what He wants to show you until after you've resumed eating. Since fasting opens your perception of the spirit world, you may hear other spirits too.

If you doubt the importance of fasting, take note that to endure Satan's temptation in the wilderness **Jesus** went on a forty day fast!

Fasting may foster a single solution (or even solve a problem) or be part of a compound solution. For example, during a fast you may realize something that requires action or change.

When you start eating again, don't overdo it. If you're inexperienced, eat some vegetables and rice if you've been fasting for multiple days.

Remember that your spirit and body are tied together as long as you're alive. The condition of your body affects the spirit person (your spirit) inside you. Take care of your body. I find that if I'm well physically I'm better able to resist temptation. Eating properly and exercising are important.

Never give up

Keep going forward in the Lord. As explained earlier, there are many factors that make life difficult. There will be opposition and problems, wrong spirit trails, times when you fall; and even in God, there will be times that doubts will flood your mind. There will be times, even when following God the best you can, that the rug will be pulled out from under you.

Lift yourself up with faith in God and His provision and *go forward*. *Work hard* at what you do, do the best you can to resist sin (and ask God to deliver you from sin you can't resist), decide to be a soul winner, minister to God's people, be kind and respectful, extend love, refuse to be incapacitated, be productive, be humble, be forgiving – **and go forward**. There may be great hardship and, depending on your situation, there may be risk, even great risk. If you find yourself in a situation where the only way forward is with risk (even great risk), do it -- otherwise you may well find yourself in economic or other poverty, or perhaps at a dead end.

The following is a template for not giving up. It may not

pertain to your situation, but it's a good example of not giving up under discouragement and hardship.

I recently went to a Sunday service in a church I used to attend. It had been a start up church headed by a couple in their late fifties. He had been a worship leader but not a pastor. He had spent much of his working life cleaning carpets. He often stated that God had told them to raise up the work.

The church was just OK; the preaching was weak and some management skills were lacking. The man's wife was on some kind of anti-depressant (or other prescription drug) and at times out to lunch. For now-obvious reasons, I wasn't so sure that this start-up church work was actually of God. Because of the fellow's poor management skills, his wife's behavior, and a change in my residence, I left the church.

During my recent visit I found that the church had doubled in size and the preaching was good, even prophetic. I also noted that the marriage and unity of the pastor and his wife were strong – and she was *well*. The pastor spoke of the multiple times the rug had been pulled out from under them. I realized that, in fact, God *had* called them and that they had continued on during great difficulty, and they, in God, had established a good and growing church. And the message he preached? "Never give up."

My son is younger. He is ordained with the Assemblies of God and has a large support network. He is very well trained in ministry: he was raised where we operated a Christian family center for the needy, attended an Assembly of God university, and served as an intern and assistant in large, growing, healthy churches. He took a small church and in short order tripled its size and started a building campaign. My son is young, energetic and the age of a domestic mission pastor.

My pastor friend (referred to above) is beyond the age where most people start a church. He was without formal pastoral training and without denominational support. He went out on his own, directed by God, with *minimal* support and backing.

So you see? God works in all ways, through traditional training and by calling people without skills, support, or recognition.

Regardless of your situation, dream God's dream for you and go forward. **Never give up. Keep this book near and apply the principles as you go forward**. Although I am not strong enough to minister to you personally, you have *no idea* how much I want to help you be all that God wants you to be and accomplish all that God has for you to do. This book is for you from God's and my heart.

Risk and impossibility

God sees things much differently than we do. The Bible says "nothing is impossible for God." When God looks at a task, He sees *how* to do it; *to Him, impossibility doesn't exist*. By contrast, human beings look at people and circumstances to determine *if* a task is possible.

Sooner or later, God always does the impossible. I've lived it. Here's but a puny example from my collection, but one that involves easy-to-understand physics. In an ***impossibly short space***, God stopped a van I was driving (at 35 mph on a dirt road) to keep me from hitting a man on a bicycle. The tires did not skid, there was no rapid deceleration, there were no panic brakes— the van just stopped ¼" from the man. There is ***no way***, in the natural world that I could have pulled off this miracle.

The Bible is filled with impossibilities. Here are just a few of them:

- Abraham and Sarah were too old to produce Isaac in the natural.
- Moses was a stuttering old shepherd when God called him to return to Egypt to lead the Israelites back to the Promised Land.
- The provision of God for Israel was impossible: food and water in the desert for millions of people ***for decades***.
- The conquest of Canaan by Israel was impossible without God's continual help.

NOTE: The conquest of Canaan is also about judgment on its inhabitants: God judges and punishes sin. Deal with it. It is real. God is God and He sets the rules and punishment.

The list goes on and on. In fact, from what I can see, any time God is serious, He will ALWAYS do the impossible at some point. By doing the impossible, He attests that He is God and that He is into the event or the calling.

The point is that in your experience, walk, and calling with God you will come up against the impossible. It doesn't mean that God does not love you; it means that God is calling you to trust him and go forward to do the impossible. ***Doing the "impossible"*** often is the only way for God to achieve His plan. In a seemingly impossible situation, you have two choices: go on with God into the "impossible", or surrender to what you believe is "possible" and never fulfill the major purpose that God has for your life.

I've lived the impossible. Twice in my life I've been disabled, but wasn't. More times than I can count I've come up against a brick wall—no way over, under, around or through—and God directed me somewhere else: to "His way." But His "way" was *extremely* risky; I even deemed it *unwise*; I had **no** peace about taking that road. It seemed God's escape for me was across a solid rock wall with minimal handholds and a thousand feet of rock cliff below...ending in more rocks. ***And I made it anyway***!

As the pastor said, "Never give up." Go on with God. If there is only one road open, no matter how absurd, take it. If there are multiple roads, be wise, be safe unless God directs otherwise and confirms the direction through several mature Christian people. But know this: God has no limits. He chooses as He decides.

God wants to do great things in your life and in the lives of your loved ones, but that will only happen by trusting Him and going into the supernatural in whatever measure is necessary to accomplish the purposes of God...and your own. You must move forward in God; that's your job. God will do the rest. Trust is the answer to the fear you'll feel. Never give up, and never give up on yourself. Trust and praising God will also bring you joy.

Walking on water

When Peter saw Jesus he said something like, if that is you, tell me to walk on the water...and Peter did until he looked at the waves, then he began to sink (Matthew 14:28–30).

A couple of points: the supernatural is very real; it overcomes the natural. The second: When Jesus tells you to come to Him on the water of your life, WALK. Just do it. As Jesus made a way for Peter to walk on the water, He will make a way for you to walk on the nothingness of your life. You don't get it, but I am walking on water to write this book for you. In fact I am living to teach you what you need to know to enter into the abundant life that Jesus has for you.

Final comments: Spirit vs. spirit power.

The battle is all about spirit vs. Spirit power. God has given us His Spirit power to win over the spirit power of the enemy. As explained, you live in an awful fallen environment with many enemies that you cannot see. This book is about principles and steps to help you navigate through the seen and unseen worlds. Use them. Remember always that God's most important provision for you is based on what Jesus did by dying on the cross; embrace the full benefit of what He did. Use the tools and resources laid out in this book and draw close to Jesus; put your roots into Jesus (Col. 2:6 & 7). Be friends with Him and embrace the life He died to give you. And remember, life here will never be perfect, so don't be discouraged when you lose battles – or when you are in a long battle that seems to being going against you. Keep going forward. God sees your struggles and is rooting for you. He really *does* love you.

I look forward to seeing you at the Great Party in Heaven.

Ciao, Brother and Fellow Traveler, Timothy

For more teaching on
"How to Defeat Your Saboteurs"
see the blog attached to the book's website at:
www.lifeabundant.net

Need additional copies?

To order more copies of

contact NewBookPublishing.com

❐ Order online at NewBookPublishing.com/ Bookstore

❐ Call 877-311-5100 or

❐ Email Info@NewBookPublishing.com

Reliance Media